■SCHOLASTIC

Fresh Takes on Centers

READING COMPREHENSION

MARY BETH ALLEN

New York • Toronto • London • Auckland • Sydney
Mexico City • New Delhi • Hong Kong • Buenos Aires

Teaching *Resources*

To Rich and Lynnette

Cover design: Jason Robinson

Interior design: Holly Grundon

Interior illustrations: bhg GRAPHIC DESIGN

Text copyright © 2010 by Mary Beth Allen

Illustrations copyright © 2010 by Scholastic Inc.

ISBN-13: 978-0-439-92921-9

ISBN-10: 0-439-92921-0

Published by Scholastic Inc.

1 2 3 4 5 6 7 8 9 10   40   17 16 15 14 13 12 11 10

Contents

Introduction

Getting Ready for Centers

Reproducible Charts, Contracts, and Assessments

Centers

Fluency Center

Independent Reading Center

Vocabulary Center

References

Introduction

Comprehension is the goal of reading, and readers construct meaning as they read texts that give them new experiences, introduce them to new characters, and provide them with new information. The National Reading Panel (NICHHD, 2000) defined the major components of reading as phonemic awareness, phonics, fluency, comprehension, and vocabulary. The panel report recommended not only the direct teaching of these components, but also ample time for students to practice so they can become competent in each one. The more children read, the better adept at reading for meaning they become, so it is important that classrooms are set up to include many opportunities to practice reading and writing. Reading comprehension centers provide a great way for students to practice all of the comprehension skills and strategies that have been taught in whole- and small-group lessons.

An Overview

Fresh Takes on Centers: Reading Comprehension provides lessons and activities for implementing yearlong centers for fluency, independent reading, and vocabulary. These research-based centers and activities are designed to provide the repeated practice students need to develop the skills and strategies of competent readers. Following is an overview of each of the reading comprehension centers.

Fluency Center (pages 30–74): Fluency is the ability to read with expression and appropriate pacing. Fluency—both in silent and oral reading—is important because it allows readers to focus on understanding the text, rather than on decoding. Activities in this section engage students in reading aloud—individually, with partners, and in small groups—and in using rubrics to evaluate the components of fluency and set goals for improvement.

Independent Reading Center (pages 75–133): This center is set up to encourage students to read widely on their own, practicing the skills and strategies that have been taught in read-aloud and guided settings. Activities in this section invite students to document their thinking before, during, and after reading.

Vocabulary Center (pages 134–190): The activities at this center make vocabulary practice playful and fun, and help students expand their word knowledge as they use graphic organizers, games, and other reproducible pages.

Each of the three center sections features sets of ready-to-use activity pages that include the following components.

✤ **Setting Up the Center:** An overview of each center includes a listing of connections to the language arts standards, a comprehensive materials list, a mini-lesson for preparing students for working independently at the center, and suggestions for differentiated learning.

✤ **Teacher Pages:** A Materials list makes it easy to determine at a glance what you need to create and set up the center. Step-by-step instructions for introducing the center (Procedures for Teaching) are designed to help you show students how to work independently at the center. Suggestions and tips for providing further support and challenges make it easy to adapt the center activities to meet the varied needs of your students.

✤ **Student Pages:** A student directions page includes a checklist (What You Need) to help students get organized for working at the center and encourages independence. This page also provides step-by-step directions (What to Do) to guide students in successfully completing center activities. You will want to laminate this reusable page for durability. Reproducible center activity pages include rubrics, record sheets, game boards, manipulatives, graphic organizers, and more.

To successfully implement reading comprehension centers in the classroom, it is important to consider the components of effective comprehension instruction. Following is a research-based overview of both instruction and practice, with specifics on how to integrate comprehension centers into your literacy program to support students in becoming competent and capable readers.

Reading Instruction and Practice

The best teachers of reading understand that instruction and practice take place in many contexts. According to Gambrell, Malloy, and Mazzoni (2007), successful teachers use a combination of instructional practices and a mix of whole-group, small-group, and individual instruction. Allington (2005) offers multiple group settings, including whole-group, small-group, and side-by-side, as part of an effective literacy program. To incorporate a balance of instructional and practice contexts, teachers will often use read-aloud and shared reading to provide

Teaching ↘ TIP

Suggestions for differentiated learning are provided in the setup section for each center (pages 32, 79, and 136) and for each individual center activity. Use these suggestions to adapt activities in order to provide students with more support or greater challenge.

instruction, guided reading for scaffolded practice, and many opportunities for independent practice. Good teachers also craft an intricate mix of direct instruction with guided and independent practice so their students are engaged in reading and thinking throughout most of the designated literacy time. (See Teaching Reading: A Framework for Instruction and Practice, below.)

Teaching Reading: A Framework for Instruction and Practice

Direct Instruction

Context: Teacher-directed read-aloud or shared reading and thinking aloud

Focus: Modeled use of phonemic awareness, phonics, fluency, vocabulary, and/or comprehension skills and strategies

Texts: Interesting, age-appropriate, and useful for teaching the skills or strategies

Practice

Guided

Context: Small groups of students reading with teacher support

Focus: Previously taught skills and strategies

Texts: Instructional level, interesting, and age-appropriate

Independent

Context: Students reading on their own

Focus: Previously taught skills and strategies

Texts: Independent level, interesting, age-appropriate

Guided Reading/Comprehension

- Teacher introduces new text or reviews familiar text
- Teacher reviews the skills or strategies to be used for this text
- Students read a portion of the text, and teacher guides students' use of the skills or strategies
- Teacher listens in or observes students while they are reading to check for fluency and strategy use
- Teacher guides students to share ideas they have about the text by using the strategies; teacher scaffolds reading or thinking as needed
- Process continues until students successfully demonstrate use of skills or strategies
- Students continue to read and apply the skills or strategies

Centers/ Independent Work Areas

- Fluency
- Independent Reading
- Vocabulary

Reading Practice

- Independent
- Buddy
- Literature Circles
- Independent Projects

Summarize Learning, Reflect, and Set Goals

Read-Aloud/Shared Reading

Reading aloud to students is a necessary part of effective literacy instruction. This context provides the most reading support for students yet allows them to engage in the thinking of competent readers. During a read-aloud setting, the teacher reads from a trade book, poem, magazine article, or textbook selection and engages students in the thinking needed to make sense of the text. The process for teaching the strategies in this context includes the following:

✤ Explaining the strategies and the processes that will be used to apply the strategy

✤ Demonstrating the use of the strategy, including the thinking and documenting process

✤ Providing guided practice using prompts and cues, with gradual release of responsibility to students as they demonstrate competency

✤ Providing independent practice in small groups, pairs, or individually

✤ Summarizing the learning and the thinking, and setting goals for future application

This context allows teachers to show students how to think like competent readers and then lead them into using that thinking by scaffolding with sections of texts. You can carefully observe students' thinking through their comments, writing, and drawing and can release the responsibility to the students as they demonstrate understanding.

Guided Practice

In this context, students are reading an instructional-level text and the teacher is scaffolding their thinking. The scaffolding happens by reviewing the previously taught strategies and processes, and then sectioning the text as a way to guide students through reading and thinking about the text, while applying the strategies that they have been taught in the read-aloud setting. The key to the guided-practice setting is that as students are reading, they are supported in their use of comprehension strategies.

Several educators recommend small, guided groups as a way to meet the individual needs of readers (Fountas & Pinnell, 1996; McLaughlin & Allen, 2002; Diller, 2007; Tyner & Green, 2005). When working with small groups, you can choose texts that are at the instructional level of the readers. Within this context, students have a little challenge, yet the guided setting provides lots of support for practicing the word identification and comprehension skills and strategies they have learned.

Independent Practice

Once students have demonstrated that they can use the comprehension strategies and document their thinking using the processes they've been taught, they can start to apply this in independent contexts. The independent setting may be small groups, pairs, or individuals, and can include special reading assignments or comprehension centers. It is through the use of these independent contexts that the students get to take ownership of the thinking that successful readers use. Teachers need to carefully incorporate the use of such independent contexts as a way of ensuring that a great deal of practice at appropriate reading and thinking levels is taking place.

Teaching for Comprehension: How to Teach

Although the goal of reading is comprehension, effective comprehension instruction is often a challenge for teachers to plan and implement. This may be due to several factors. First, there are so many district and state standards and outcomes to address that teachers need to cover a vast amount of information in a short time. Too often this causes comprehension to become a way to assess understanding after reading, and not necessarily to be the focus of the reading instruction. Pressley, Wharton-McDonald, Hampston, & Echevarria (1998) found that although teachers believed they were teaching comprehension, what the researchers observed was the mentioning, assigning, and assessing of comprehension, not necessarily its *instruction*. This was similar to what Durkin (1978–1979) found 20 years earlier, with comprehension being *assessed* most often and taught rarely. Another challenge is that with a focus on research-based published programs, there are too many choices in the teacher's manuals, and they often focus on discreet sub-skills of reading, minimizing the thinking that readers may construct as they engage with text. Additionally, there is often a time constraint for finishing a selection, and with multiple skills covered within the selection, little time remains to teach students to think through the text. Finally, the high-stakes tests that are a part of all grade levels provide a barrier to comprehension instruction. Multiple-choice responses and standardized responses to prompts yield teaching that is rote, routine, and basic.

Although there are challenges to implementing effective comprehension instruction, there is, happily, strong support for the planning and teaching of comprehension. Accomplished teachers provide modeled instruction and extensive coaching to guide students to think like competent readers (Duke & Pearson, 2002; Fielding & Pearson, 1994; McLaughlin & Allen, 2002; Reutzel, Smith, & Fawson, 2005). The orchestration of direct instruction, teacher modeling, and coaching decisions is a complex process. Commonalities observed among reading experts are that the instruction include direct teacher modeling through reading aloud and thinking aloud, guided practice using instructional or independent texts with a gradual release of responsibility to the students, and, finally, lots of independent practice, with students taking more and more ownership of using comprehension strategies. Additionally, the National Reading Panel (NICHHD, 2000) recommended a variety of instructional practices that teachers can use to support readers as they try to make meaning of text. These include comprehension monitoring, cooperative learning, using graphic and semantic organizers, asking and answering questions, using story structure, and summarizing text. Comprehension centers provide an excellent venue for practicing what has been taught in modeled and guided settings.

Teaching for Comprehension: What to Teach

Comprehension strategies and skills can and should be taught. Good readers are strategic and use all the information stored in their brains, (from prior experiences and reading) to make connections to the current reading. These connections allow readers to use the strategies to make sense of the text. There are several strategies and skills that readers use before, during, and after reading that help them engage with the text and construct meaning. Although there is agreement that this is what readers do, there is not one standard list of strategies that all experts agree upon.

Harvey and Goudvis (2007) suggest readers use six strategies: activating background knowledge and making connections; questioning; making inferences; visualizing; determining importance; and summarizing and synthesizing information. Keene and Zimmermann (2007) concur, and add using sensory images and monitoring for meaning. McLaughlin and Allen (2002) made a list of eight strategies: previewing, connecting, self-questioning, visualizing, monitoring, knowing how words work, summarizing, and evaluating. Some researchers suggest a set of strategies taught as a group to help readers actively make meaning. Reutzel, Smith, and Fawson (2005) suggest teaching the following strategies: activating background knowledge, text structure, predicting, asking questions, goal setting, imagery, monitoring, and summarizing. Brown (2008) recommends making connections, predicting, visualizing, self-questioning, summarizing, and clarifying as the set of strategies readers use to make meaning from text.

Following is a list of strategies that successful readers use. Each of these can be modeled through read-aloud or shared reading settings, scaffolded within guided settings, and practiced in independent settings, such as comprehension centers.

Activating Prior Knowledge: Thinking about what is already known about the text or topic; this gets the reader's mind ready to read and think about the text, and to make the connections necessary to construct meaning

Predicting: Making connections with the text in order to make guesses about the content presented and about what might happen; this provides an impetus to keep reading—to find out or get more clues and revise predictions

Setting Purposes for Reading: Being aware of the reason for reading and the types of strategies needed to meet that goal

Identifying Text Structure: Deciding what type of text is being read and how it is organized to communicate the message; this can influence both purpose and strategies for reading

Inferring: Using text clues and reader clues to draw conclusions about the story and characters; reading "between the lines" or "beyond the text"

Asking and Answering Questions: Generating questions to guide reading; this provides a reason to read (to answer the questions) and encourages readers to generate new questions as more clues are obtained

Visualizing/Sensing: Tapping into the senses and creating mental pictures and other sensory images while reading the text; becoming part of the text and using the mind's eye

Identifying Important Information: Making decisions while reading about what is most important and worth remembering; being able to summarize important content during and after reading

Monitoring and Clarifying: Asking "Does this make sense?" and clarifying by adapting strategic processes to accommodate the response; using a variety of strategies to construct meaning and, when meaning is disrupted, using one or more fix-up strategies to get meaning

Summarizing: Recalling important information and synthesizing those ideas; being able to retell or encapsulate the key information in one's own words

Evaluating: Making decisions about the quality or effectiveness of the text and writing, about the characters and the content of the text, and about themselves as readers

Regardless of the particular set of strategies, educators agree that reading is more than just reading words as quickly as possible. Reading is about the meaning that a reader constructs by making connections with the print and existing understandings. If the goal is to teach students to think while they read, then the teaching must focus on what good readers do and how they do it. This should be supported by providing many opportunities for students to practice with texts that they can read and want to read (Estes & Johnstone, 1977). Comprehension centers provide an effective context for allowing that to happen on a regular basis. For a summary of teaching practices, see Teaching Comprehension, below.

Teaching Comprehension

How to Teach

Explain
Explain the strategies and the process, what kind of thinking to use, and why it is important.

Model
Model the strategies and the process, using a read-aloud and a think-aloud to demonstrate how to think like an effective reader and how to document that thinking. Both the thinking and the reason for the thinking (text and reader factors) need to be shared.

Guided Practice
Guide students in applying the strategies, gradually releasing the responsibility to the students as they demonstrate understanding. Provide hints or prompts as needed to guide thinking.

Independent Practice
Provide opportunities for students to practice using the strategies in groups, pairs, or independently.

Summarize, Reflect, and Set Goals
Summarize the learning, reflect on the use of the strategies, and set goals for applying the strategies in new contexts.

What to Teach

Before Reading Strategies (Anticipating)
Activating prior knowledge
Predicting
Setting purposes for reading
Asking questions
Identifying text type and purpose

During Reading Strategies (Constructing Meaning)
Visualizing/sensing
Monitoring and clarifying
Asking and answering questions
Identifying important information
Synthesizing and summarizing information
Making inferences
Revising predictions

After Reading Strategies (Reflecting)
Summarizing
Evaluating
Extending learning
Asking and answering questions

Getting Ready
for Centers

There is a plethora of research to support the teaching of reading using a mix of large-group, small-group, and individual contexts. Allington (2005) recommends a combination of the three types of instruction to best meet the needs of all students. Similarly, Gambrell, Malloy, and Mazzoni (2007) suggest that the most effective teachers use a mix of instructional formats. Depending on the time frames and goals of your district or classroom, you may choose an existing framework or create one of your own. Regardless of how you structure your literacy block, it is important that students get a balance of instruction, guided practice, and independent practice. Centers provide an excellent context for independent practice while you are working with small groups of students.

Introducing the Centers

Centers provide a time for students to practice skills and strategies that have been previously taught. There should be nothing that students are asked to do at centers that they have not been taught how to do; however, it is certainly an ideal time for students to apply skills and strategies to new contexts.

When introducing centers to students, start small and add on as students become accustomed to working independently. An important consideration when introducing a center is to model how to work through the directions, how to use the materials, what to do with work that is complete or in progress, and how to self-assess using the rubrics.

To help students get ready for the routines and procedures necessary for successful implementation of centers, use the first four to six weeks of school to develop routines and frameworks. This is a good use of literacy time while you are gathering assessment data for grouping students. Start by explaining procedures to students and introducing the work board or other structure you will use to schedule and manage center time. (See page 13 for more information, also pages 21–26 for a variety of work board formats.) Review expectations for independent work, such as what students should do if they need help, the appropriate voice level, and what procedures to follow when the work is completed.

To get started with implementing centers, divide the class into two groups and introduce one center activity. Using your work board to organize this (see Organizing and Implementing Center Choices, page 14), have one group work on the center activity while the other group works with you in a guided setting. After a set amount of time (10–20 minutes), switch groups. Following this first session, engage students in a discussion about how things went. Focus on the rules, the work completed, and the noise level. Repeat this process for about a week, or until students seem to understand how to use the work board, work independently, and solve their own problems.

Next, divide the class into three groups. Introduce one or two more centers and, using the work board, organize students to work at the centers or with you. Work with a group for a set amount of time (10–20 minutes), then take another group to work with you and have remaining students work at a center. Repeat until each group has worked with you and at each center. After the session, discuss with the students what worked and what they can improve upon. Help them decide what they need to do the next day to make it a more successful experience. Adapt as necessary. Repeat this process for about a week, or until the students can handle this level of independence. Next, try the same process with four groups or start full implementation with multiple guided-reading groups.

The advantages of starting off slowly this way are many. First, before utilizing small-group instruction and practice, a variety of strategies and processes for documenting thinking can be taught during read-alouds. Any of the processes that are taught during this time will be available to students during center time. Another advantage is that it helps students learn how to work independently and use the work board. Additionally, this gives you time to assess students' reading levels in order to form guided-reading groups. By the time the class is ready for full implementation, students should be very familiar with the process, the expectations, and the work they need to do at the centers.

Teaching TIP

The concept of a "work board" was introduced by Fountas and Pinnell (1996) as a way to manage independent work with a set of routine tasks. A work board is a visual display that includes students' names (or group names), names (or graphics) representing the tasks, and a rotation schedule.

Forming Groups

One of the benefits of teaching with small groups is that it allows teachers to meet with groups that have similar interests, needs, or reading levels. Therefore, it is important to gather information about students prior to implementing small-group instruction—for example, through individual conferences or by using an "interest inventory" to learn about students' hobbies, reading preferences, time spent reading, perceptions about themselves as readers, and attitudes about reading.

Additionally, finding students' approximate reading level using an oral reading assessment with an analysis of miscues and a comprehension evaluation will help with group formation and lesson goals. This can be done by having students read leveled classroom texts aloud, recording and analyzing all miscues, and asking text-based and inferential questions. Students can also write a summary of what they have read, which provides valuable information about comprehension. The writing sample can also be evaluated for writing abilities, including focus, content, organization, word choice, sentence structure, and mechanics.

Another way to gather data about students is to use an assessment kit. Most of the published assessment kits include leveled readers, scoring sheets to record and analyze miscues, comprehension questions, and writing prompts. Some good published assessment tools include *Developmental Reading Assessments 2* (Beaver, 2006; Beaver & Carter, 2003), *Fountas and Pinnell Benchmark Assessment System* (Fountas & Pinnell, 2007), and the *Rigby Benchmark Assessment Kit*.

After information is gathered about students, their levels, their preferences, and their interests, lessons can be planned, books can be chosen, and centers can be created. Each of these can be implemented to meet the needs and levels of each student in the class.

Organizing and Implementing Center Choices

There are various options for managing students' movement to centers, each with different benefits. It is best to choose one that works with the organizational preferences of the teacher and the learning styles of the students, and then it is important to be consistent in holding students accountable for the work they produce and their time on task in the centers.

A work board (or center chart) provides a visual display of the centers and who should be at the centers. Work boards help you manage students by providing a visual organization of who will work at each center. They help students by providing a reminder of where they need to be and when, which minimizes interruptions during guided reading. To create a work board, list all the centers and provide a visual icon of each, if possible. Next, leave a space for group names, student names, or student pictures. If the centers are teacher managed and directed, then you should move names or pictures each day to indicate where students need to be. This can be set up for one or more time segments. Another way to use the work board is to place students' names at the center where they will start and then let students move their names as they finish work at a center. The work board provides a good visual reminder for students of where they need to be and can also help you know, at a glance, where students are or should be. An overview of several options for organizing center choices and setting up work boards follows.

Teacher-Directed Center Management

Using this system, teachers set up the schedule to tell students where they need to go at what time. The guided-reading group can be included in the rotation, or teachers can call students during each time slot to work in the group. When using this system, it is important to create activities that can be completed in the allotted time. The following samples show options for organizing a center-rotation schedule according to this approach.

Center Rotation Chart (1): Fill in students' names for each group to assign centers for each time block. (See template, page 21.)

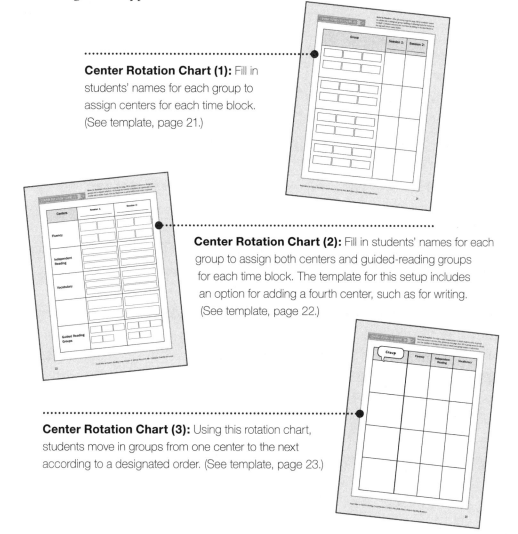

Center Rotation Chart (2): Fill in students' names for each group to assign both centers and guided-reading groups for each time block. The template for this setup includes an option for adding a fourth center, such as for writing. (See template, page 22.)

Center Rotation Chart (3): Using this rotation chart, students move in groups from one center to the next according to a designated order. (See template, page 23.)

Teaching ↘ **TIP**

A typical classroom center setup may include both reading and writing centers. *Fresh Takes on Centers: Writing* by Mary Beth Allen (Scholastic, 2010) is a companion to this book and features writing center activities.

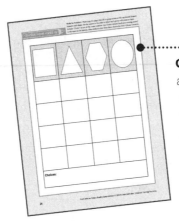

Centers Work Board (1): Simple graphics, such as shapes, provide a quick visual reminder of where students in each group should be. This chart builds a "Choices" option into the rotation schedule. (See template, page 24.)

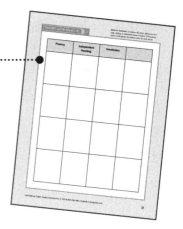

Centers Work Board (2): This work board uses group names (such as colors) to designate the order of rotation for each center. The template for this setup includes an option for adding an additional center, such as for writing. (See template, page 25.)

Student-Directed Center Management

Another option for managing centers is to let students choose where they will go each day. This can take a lot of the responsibility off of the teacher and place it on students. For this to work, though, several structures need to be in place. First, there must be clear expectations about what students need to accomplish within the time frame of the centers. In other words, if the expectation is that they need to visit each center within a one- or two-week time frame, students need to understand this goal and know they will be accountable for the work they produce at each center. Second, students need to know how many classmates can be at a center at one time. This can easily be accomplished by posting a number at the center or by having a certain number of spaces where students can fill in their names. Third, there needs to be an organizational system so students know who will select which centers first. This can be rotated, or students can start the next day at the same center they were working at the previous day. Regardless of the system, students need to know that they can move to another center only when their work is finished, and can only go to a center that has spaces available.

A Center Sign-Up Chart provides a record of students' center work. (See sample, below.) When students choose a particular center, they check off their name on a chart underneath the day they are working there. Discuss parameters about how often students can work at a center to ensure students get to each center.

Center Sign-Up Chart: A sign-up chart makes it easy to see, at a glance, which centers students have completed, so that reminders can be given as needed. Photocopy and customize the Center Sign-Up Chart for use at each center. (See template, page 26. Fill in the center name in the space provided at the top.)

Organizing Center Materials and Space

A "center" is a concept more than a place, and to encourage students to work independently, it is important to provide systems for organizing materials. Following are suggestions for organizing both center materials and students' work.

Organizing Materials

Make decisions on the physical display of centers based on available classroom space and the needs of students. Although it is optimum to have students moving and working with other students, this does not need to take up a lot of space in the classroom. Each center must have clear directions, resources, activity sheets, samples, and rubrics. These may be housed in pocket folders, plastic bins, plastic drawers, gift bags, pizza boxes, bulletin boards, closet doors, or plastic bags. The important thing to remember is that while students need to be able to work at the center independently, that may mean they take the directions and materials back to their desks. Suggestions for both portable and designated center-area setups follow.

> **Portable Pocket-Folder Centers:** If students are taking center materials back to their desks, stock pocket folders with necessary supplies, placing student directions on the left, and the corresponding center activity sheet on the right. Label the front of the pocket folder for easy identification. Other options for creating portable centers include gift bags (with handles), plastic bins, and shoe boxes.

Center Area Setup: If students are working at a designated center area (such as a work table), fill baskets or boxes with sets of materials. Laminate student directions and rubrics for durability. Store supplies of center activity pages in folders, with a copy stapled to the front for easy identification. Stock the center with pens, pencils, and other necessary supplies (which may vary depending on the activity).

Organizing Student Work

Students can keep track of their work during center time with a two-pocket folder. One side of the folder can hold an individual checklist that students can use to keep track of the centers they have visited each day and their completed work. (See sample, below.) The pocket on the other side can hold work in progress. Students can store their folders in their desks or in a separate center bin.

Individual Center Sheet: This chart encourages time management and organization skills. Customize this page to include additional centers if desired. (See template, page 27.)

Accountability and Assessment

Whether work is completed individually, in pairs, or in small groups, it is important that students are responsible for their time while working at centers. Therefore, systems for accountability must be in place as part of the planning.

Amount of Work

For each center, think about what students should accomplish. For example, an independent reading center may require that a certain amount of reading be completed and that students document something related to their reading that day. It may be as simple as recording the book title and number of pages read or writing a summary in a reading journal.

Some teachers create student contracts that list all the centers and specific work that needs to be accomplished at each. The contract may be for a week or more; students then know what needs to be completed and when. (See sample, below.) You may guide students in completing the Activity/Goal section for each center (or complete it for them in advance).

Centers Contract: Students can store their Centers Contract in their folders (see Organizing Student Work, page 18) for a handy reminder of expectations at each center. Customize this page to include additional centers if desired. (See template, page 28.)

Summative Assessments

Although center work is important evidence of what students are learning and capable of doing independently, it would be very difficult to grade every center activity. Instead, choose a few pieces each week to grade. One way to do this is to identify one piece that is required to be graded and then let students choose one that they want graded. Another way to obtain a grade is to collect all pieces completed and give students a score for work completed, and then score one or two more pieces for quality of work.

Students can also evaluate their own progress and performance for center-time activities using clearly written rubrics and self-assessments. In addition to the generic Student Self-Reflection Form (page 29), you'll find rubrics and self-assessments in each center section. (See samples, below.) On a daily, weekly, or other time basis, students can summarize what they have accomplished at the center, and what they hope to work on the next time. This serves two purposes. First, it communicates to students that center time is work time, and each day something needs to be accomplished. Second, it gives the teacher concrete documentation of student progress and provides information as to whether more student support is needed. Model using these tools in advance of center work and display them at the centers as a reminder of expectations.

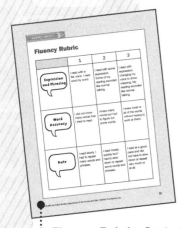

Independent Reading Center Self-Assessment: Students can use the Independent Reading Center Self-Assessment to evaluate their use of comprehension strategies and to set goals for continued improvement. (See template, page 80.)

Fluency Rubric: Students can use the Fluency Rubric to assess their progress as they practice the components of fluency, including expression and phrasing, word accuracy, and rate. This rubric also encourages students to set goals for further practice. (See template, page 33.)

Vocabulary Center Self-Assessment: This Vocabulary Center Self-Assessment helps students set goals for improving word knowledge as they read, including the use of reference tools, as needed, to determine meaning. (See template, page 137.)

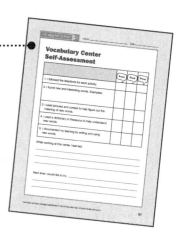

Center time is a time of practice. It can add value to any instructional model that includes small group settings. This time can be very productive and will help students gain competency in reading and writing if the time is well-organized and well-planned. Thinking through center choices, management systems, and student accountability will help you plan experiences that maximize student time and tasks, and, therefore, learning.

Note to Teacher: After photocopying this page, fill in students' names in column one to designate groups (adding or deleting boxes for names as needed). Complete columns two and three by filling in the time blocks at the top and center names below.

Group	Session 1: _____	Session 2: _____

Note to Teacher: After photocopying this page, fill in students' names to designate groups and a rotation schedule. To change the number of students at a particular center, simply add or delete boxes. Use the blank row to add an additional center if desired.

Centers	Session 1: _____	Session 2: _____
Fluency		
Independent Reading		
Vocabulary		
Guided Reading Groups		

Note to Teacher: To create a center rotation chart in which students move in groups from one center to the next, first, photocopy this page. Then, fill in group names in column one. Use numbers to designate the order in which each group rotates to each center.

Group	Fluency	Independent Reading	Vocabulary

Note to Teacher: Photocopy this page, then fill in group names at the top (inside shapes). Beneath each shape, list the centers in the order in which each group will rotate to them. Include "Choice" as one of the center rotations. List Choice options (such as a writing center) in the space at the bottom. Have students select from these choices for their "Choice" rotation.

Choices:			

Note to Teacher: To prepare this chart, photocopy this page, adding an additional center if desired. Fill in group names to designate the rotation order for each center.

Fluency	Independent Reading	Vocabulary	

CENTER: _____

Directions

Sign your name and check the day you worked at this center.

Name	Monday	Tuesday	Wednesday	Thursday	Friday

Note to Teacher: Customize the centers listed as needed to reflect your center setup, using the blank rows for additional centers.

Directions

Mark an ✗ next to the center you work at each day.

Center	Monday	Tuesday	Wednesday	Thursday	Friday
Fluency					
Independent Reading					
Vocabulary					

Name: _____   Date: _____

Note to Teacher: Customize the centers listed as needed to reflect your center setup, using the blank rows for additional centers.

CENTERS CONTRACT ▷

Name _____ Date _____

Directions

Write the activity or goal you will work on next to the center name. When you finish the activity at the center, write the date in the Date Completed column. Turn in the contract and all work on

_____ .
   Due Date

Center	Activity/Goal	Date Completed
Fluency		
Independent Reading		
Vocabulary		

_____
Student Signature

_____
Teacher Signature

STUDENT SELF-REFLECTION FORM

Name: ______________________ Date: ______________

Center: ______________________________________

Description of the work I completed at this center . . .

____

____

____

____

Evidence . . .

____

____

____

What I did well . . .

____

____

____

____

My new goal is . . .

____

____

____

____

Teaching ↘ TIP

To keep this center going throughout the entire year, change texts, activities, partners and groups, or focus of practice to maintain interest and an appropriate level of difficulty.

Setting Up a Fluency Center

Fluency is one of the major components identified by the National Reading Panel (NICHHD, 2000) and is necessary for successful reading and comprehension. Fluency—the ability to read text accurately, quickly, and with appropriate expression—is necessary so that readers can devote most of their attention to meaning, not word recognition. The purpose of the Fluency Center is to give students the opportunity to practice reading and rereading texts so they can become more fluid and expressive. Working at the Fluency Center, students practice word automaticity, phrasing, expression, and rate. By providing activities that help students read and reread texts, sometimes performing that reading for others, students become more fluent in their reading, and therefore understand the text better. The Fluency Center provides many opportunities to practice the components of fluency in a fun yet meaningful way.

Connections to the Standards

The center activities in this section support the following standards for students in grades 3–5, outlined by Mid-continent Research for Education and Learning (McREL), an organization that collects and synthesizes national and state K–12 curriculum standards.

Reading
Uses the general skills and strategies of the reading process
- Previews text, for example, by skimming and using text format
- Establishes a purpose for reading
- Uses phonetic and structural analysis techniques, syntactic structure, and semantic context to decode unknown words
- Use a variety of context clues to decode unknown words
- Understands level-appropriate reading vocabulary
- Monitors own reading strategies and makes modifications as needed
- Adjusts speed of reading to suit purpose and difficulty of the material
- Uses personal criteria, such as interest or text difficulty, to select reading material

Uses reading skills and strategies to understand and interpret a variety of literary texts
- Understands the ways in which language, such as alliteration, hyperbole, and rhythm, is used in literary texts
- Knows the defining characteristics of a variety of literary forms and genres
- Understands the ways in which language is used in literary texts

Listening and Speaking
Uses speaking and listening skills for different purposes
- Listens to classmates and adults
- Uses strategies to convey a clear point
- Makes basic oral presentations to class
- Uses a variety of verbal and nonverbal communication skills
- Listens for specific information in spoken texts

Source: *Content Knowledge: A Compendium of Standards and Benchmarks for K–12 Education* (4th ed.). Mid-continent Research for Education and Learning, 2004 (http://www.mcrel.org/standards–benchmarks).

Fluency Center Materials

✤ Student texts (books, poetry, short stories, and articles at independent and instructional reading levels, including those previously read)

✤ Fluency Rubric (page 33)

✤ Fluency Center Record Sheet (page 34)

✤ Additional rubrics and self-assessments

✤ Student activity pages

✤ Samples of completed activities

✤ Recording device (such as a computer)

✤ Headphones

✤ Recorded texts and print versions

✤ Sticky notes

✤ Examples of excellent work

Teaching the Process

Fluency needs to be taught and practiced. All components of fluency (automaticity, phrasing, expression, and rate) can be taught using direct instruction, and then practiced at the center. The instruction should include modeling, guiding, and gradually releasing the responsibility to the students through independent work at the center. Use the following procedure to make sure all your students can work successfully at the Fluency Center.

1. Choose a familiar student text and demonstrate how fluent reading sounds. Explain to students what the components of fluent reading are and demonstrate each one. Read a text aloud, with and without good expression, phrasing, and rate. Help students become aware of what each component sounds like with fluent reading.

2. Show students the Fluency Rubric and discuss each component. Read a selection aloud and guide students in evaluating the reading. Set a goal for rereading, and then read it again, focusing on the goal. Reevaluate, using the rubric as a guide.

3. Read another passage or short text aloud to students. Then have students read the text aloud together and evaluate with the rubric. Set a goal and reread, focusing on the goal. Reevaluate with the rubric.

Teaching
↘ TIP

As you prepare to introduce a center activity, preview the lesson (Procedures for Teaching) to determine the amount of time you will need to spend on the material. Many activities are best taught over a period of several days.

Teaching ↘ TIP

Have students place a copy of the Fluency Center Record Sheet (page 34) in their folder and complete it each time they finish an activity at the Fluency Center. Encourage them to review this record sheet periodically to assess progress.

4. Have partners read a text aloud to each other and evaluate with the rubric. Guide students to set goals, and then reread the text, focusing on the goal. Have them reevaluate with the rubric, completing number 5.

5. When you think students understand the components of fluency and how to evaluate oral reading using the rubric (they will use similar rubrics with other Fluency Center activities), have them try out some of the fluency activities with less guidance.

6. For independent practice at the center, review new materials as they are added, including student directions, rubrics, and record sheets so that students can successfully work on fluency alone, with a partner, or with a small group.

Throughout this process, observe students to determine if they need more or less support. If students seem to be able to engage successfully with the components of fluency and can evaluate with the rubric, then it is appropriate for them to work at the Fluency Center. For students who need more support, continue to model components of fluency and how to evaluate using the rubric, and guide students in engaging in the same until they are ready for the center activities.

Adapting the Process

With the appropriate support or challenge, all students can improve their fluency, and therefore their comprehension. Each center activity in this section includes suggestions for differentiated learning, including for students who need additional support or greater challenge. In addition, keep the following suggestions in mind when setting up and introducing center activities.

Suggestions for Differentiated Learning

Provide More Support

- Use easier texts.
- Focus on one component of fluency at a time.
- Work on high-frequency words.

Provide More Challenge

- Use more challenging texts.
- Use texts with more complex punctuation.
- Use texts with a lot of dialogue.
- Have students work with less skilled readers, offering support as needed.

Fluency Rubric

	1	2	3
Expression and Phrasing	I read with a flat voice. I read word by word.	I read with some expression. Some of my reading sounded like normal talking.	I read with expression, changing my voice to show meaning. My reading sounded like normal talking.
Word Accuracy	I did not know many words that I tried to read.	I knew many words but had to figure out some words.	I knew most or all of the words without having to work at them.
Rate	I read slowly. I had to repeat many words and phrases.	I read mostly quickly but I had to slow down or repeat some words and phrases.	I read at a good pace and did not have to slow down or repeat very much or at all.

Name _____ Date _____

Fluency Center Record Sheet

Directions: Use this chart to record the date, the text, and your scores from the Fluency Rubric. Use the Comments box to explain your score or share something you've noticed about your reading fluency.

Date	Text	Expression and Phrasing _(I focused on reading with more expression.)_	Word Accuracy _(I knew most of the words.)_	Rate _(I read at a good pace.)_	Comments

Readers Theater

Description: Students read and reread a script, and then perform it to practice fluency skills.

Materials

✤ Readers Theater scripts (multiple copies)

✤ Student directions (page 37)

✤ Readers Theater Rubric (page 38)

✤ Pinch Cards (page 39)

✤ Readers Theater Group Sheet (page 40)

Procedures for Teaching

1. Select a script and display it for students. Model reading a section of the script aloud. Display the Readers Theater Rubric and give each student a Pinch Card (with numbers 1, 2, and 3 to match the rubric scoring). Think aloud about the performance, using the criteria on the rubric as a guide. Have students "pinch" the number on their card to show the score they give to evaluate each category.

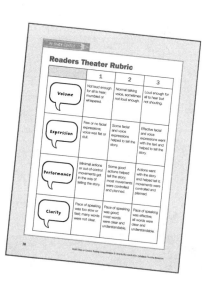

2. Reread the section, focusing on specific aspects of fluency identified by the rubric. Have students again pinch and display the number on the card to evaluate the reading. Discuss changes in the scores.

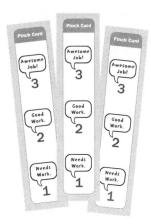

3. Now, have students join you in reading another section of the script aloud, then use the Pinch Cards and rubric to evaluate the reading. Discuss what could make the reading more expressive and interesting.

Teaching
↘ TIP

Both the Readers Theater Rubric and Pinch Cards are reusable. Laminate before placing at the center (or photocopy on cardstock) for durability.

4. Reread the section, focusing on those things. Again, using the Pinch Cards and rubric, discuss with students how the reading improves each time.

5. Allow groups of students to work on the next section of the script. Have students use the Pinch Cards and rubric to evaluate their reading. Repeat as needed to complete the script and/or allow students the opportunity to understand the process.

6. Place a variety of leveled Readers Theater scripts at the center, along with the other center materials. Review the Readers Theater Group Sheet, then group students and allow them to practice each day, using the Pinch Cards and rubric to evaluate fluency and progress. Invite groups to perform weekly or biweekly.

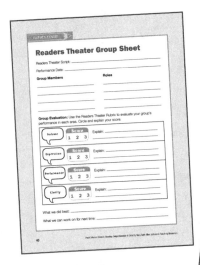

Suggestions for Differentiated Learning

Provide More Support

- Use easier scripts.

- Group struggling students with more able students to scaffold reading.

- Provide a taped version of the script for students to listen to first.

Provide More Challenge

- Use more challenging scripts.

- Encourage students to write and perform their own scripts.

- Use scripts connected to Social Studies or Science areas of study.

Fresh Takes on Centers: Reading Comprehension

Readers Theater

What to Do

1. Choose a Readers Theater script. List all group members' names on a Readers Theater Group Sheet.

2. Read through the script together. Decide who will read each part. Complete this section of the Group Sheet. Some group members may need to read more than one part.

3. Practice reading the script silently one or more times, focusing on your part.

4. Practice reading the script aloud, with each person reading his or her part. Make sure to read with good pacing and expression.

5. Evaluate the reading using the Readers Theater Rubric. You can also use the Pinch Cards to show the score. Discuss what you did best and what you can improve.

6. Practice again in preparation for reading your script to the class.

7. Use the Readers Theater Rubric to evaluate your performance, then complete the Group Sheet to tell how you did and to set goals for the next performance.

What You NEED

- ✔ Readers Theater scripts
- ✔ Readers Theater Group Sheet
- ✔ Readers Theater Rubric
- ✔ Pinch Cards

Hint! Hint!

⇒ Read the words as if you were just talking.

⇒ Use an index card under the line of text to keep your place.

⇒ Look ahead at punctuation. An exclamation mark is a reminder to show surprise or excitement in your voice. A question mark is a sign to raise the pitch of your voice at the end of the sentence. A comma is a good place to pause.

Readers Theater Rubric

	1	2	3
Volume	Not loud enough for all to hear; mumbled or whispered.	Normal talking voice, sometimes not loud enough.	Loud enough for all to hear but not shouting.
Expression	Few or no facial expressions; voice was flat or dull.	Some facial and voice expressions helped to tell the story.	Effective facial and voice expressions went with the text and helped to tell the story.
Performance	Minimal actions or out-of-control movements got in the way of telling the story.	Some good actions helped tell the story; most movements were controlled and planned.	Actions went with the story and helped tell it; movements were controlled and planned.
Clarity	Pace of speaking was too slow or fast; many words were not clear.	Pace of speaking was good; most words were clear and understandable.	Pace of speaking was effective; all words were clear and understandable.

 Fresh Takes on Centers: Reading Comprehension © 2010 by Mary Beth Allen. Scholastic Teaching Resources

Pinch Cards

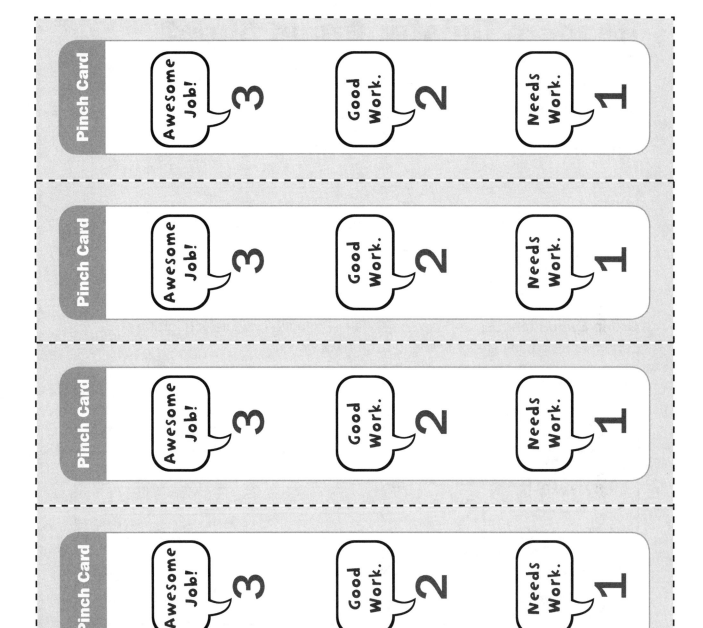

Fresh Takes on Centers: Reading Comprehension © 2010 by Mary Beth Allen. Scholastic Teaching Resources

Readers Theater Group Sheet

Readers Theater Script: _____

Performance Date: _____

Group Members   **Roles**

_____   _____

_____   _____

_____   _____

_____   _____

Group Evaluation: Use the Readers Theater Rubric to evaluate your group's performance in each area. Circle and explain your score.

	Score	Explain:
Volume	1 2 3	_____ _____
Expression	1 2 3	_____ _____
Performance	1 2 3	_____ _____
Clarity	1 2 3	_____ _____

What we did best: _____

What we can work on for next time: _____

Poetry Theater

Description: Students read and reread poems and then perform them using expression and actions.

Materials

✦ A selection of poetry

✦ Student directions (page 43)

✦ Poetry Theater Rubric (page 44)

✦ Poetry Theater Group Sheet (page 45)

✦ Pinch Cards (page 39; optional)

✦ Props (optional)

Procedures for Teaching

1. Choose and display a poem that has good action in it. Model the process of reading it aloud and thinking about how you could perform it.

2. Read the poem aloud again and perform it with expression and actions. You may incorporate small props, as well. Display the Poetry Theater Rubric and model using it to evaluate the reading. You may also use the Pinch Cards, as with Readers Theater, to involve students in evaluating the reading.

3. Display another poem and read it together. Engage students in a discussion about what actions could go with the poem. Read the poem together again and perform it with expression and actions. Use the Poetry Theater Rubric as a guide to discuss the performance.

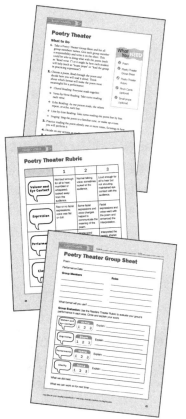

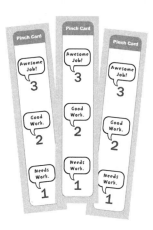

Teaching ↘ TIP

Both the Poetry Theater Rubric and Pinch Cards are reusable. Copy on cardstock, place in a plastic sleeve, or laminate for durability.

Teaching ↘ TIP

4. Explain that when everyone reads together, it's called "choral reading." Share other formats for reading aloud and demonstrate each.

✤ Verse-by-Verse Reading: Take turns reading each verse.

✤ Echo Reading: As one person (for example, a more skilled reader) reads, the group repeats, or echoes, each line.

✤ Line-by-Line Reading: Take turns reading the poem line by line.

✤ Singing: Sing the poem to a familiar or original tune.

5. Have students work in groups with a new poem. Everyone can read together chorally, or they can choose one of the other formats. Have students practice reading the poem with expression and actions, and using the rubric to evaluate each component. Invite students to share their poems with the class and have classmates evaluate the performance using the rubric and Pinch Cards.

6. Place a variety of poetry collections and copies of other poems at the center, along with the other center materials. Review the Poetry Theater Group Sheet, then group students and allow them to practice each day, using the rubric (and optional Pinch Cards) to evaluate fluency and progress. Invite groups to perform weekly or biweekly.

Suggestions for Differentiated Learning

Provide More Support

- Use poems with lines that end in rhyme to help students create rhythm in their reading.

- Provide information about key words to support expression and pacing.

- Use shorter poems or poems with more concrete interpretations.

Provide More Challenge

- Encourage use of more sophisticated clues to support fluent reading. For example, noticing alliteration can help readers sense the rhythm of a poem. Paying attention to words that go together (such as words that describe something) can help with phrasing.

- Provide thesauruses and other reference tools to build understanding of challenging language. ·

- Provide more complex poems for students to interpret and perform.

Poetry Theater

What to Do

1. Take a Poetry Theater Group Sheet and list all group members' names. Give each group member a responsibility and write it on the sheet. This could be who is doing what with the poem (such as "Read verse 1") or it might be how each student will help (such as "locate props" or "lead the group in practicing expression").

2. Choose a poem. Read through the poem and decide how you will read it aloud. Think about which format will make the poem most meaningful for a performance.

❖ Choral Reading: Everyone reads together.

❖ Verse-by-Verse Reading: Take turns reading each verse.

❖ Echo Reading: As one person reads, the others repeat, or echo, each line.

❖ Line-by-Line Reading: Take turns reading the poem line by line.

❖ Singing: Sing the poem to a familiar tune, or make up a tune.

3. Practice reading the poem silently one or more times, focusing on how you will perform it. Decide on any actions or small props. Practice reading the script aloud, using the format, the actions, and the props. Focus on reading with good pacing, phrasing, and expression.

4. Evaluate your reading using the Poetry Theater Rubric. Identify ways you can make your reading better. Practice again, focusing on areas to improve.

5. Be prepared to perform your poem for the class. After your performance, complete the Group Sheet to tell how you did and to set goals for your next performance.

What You NEED

✓ Poem

✓ Poetry Theater Group Sheet

✓ Poetry Theater Rubric

✓ Pinch Cards (optional)

✓ Small props (optional)

Poetry Theater Rubric

	1	2	3
Volume and Eye Contact	Not loud enough for all to hear; mumbled or whispered; looked away from the audience.	Normal talking voice; sometimes looked at the audience.	Loud enough for all to hear but not shouting; maintained eye contact with the audience.
Expression	Few or no facial expressions; voice was flat or dull.	Some facial expressions and voice changes helped to communicate the meaning of the poem.	Facial expressions and voice went with the poem and enhanced the interpretation.
Performance	Minimal actions or disruptive actions; shared the poem in a basic or boring way.	Some good actions helped interpret the poem; shared the poem in an interesting way.	Interpreted the poem; shared the poem in a creative and interesting way.
Clarity	Pace of speaking was too slow or fast; many words were not clear.	Pace of speaking was good; most words were clear and understandable.	Pace of speaking was effective; all words were clear and understandable.

 Fresh Takes on Centers: Reading Comprehension © 2010 by Mary Beth Allen. Scholastic Teaching Resources

Poetry Theater Group Sheet

Poem: _____

Performance Date: _____

Group Members   **Roles**

_____   _____

_____   _____

_____   _____

_____   _____

What format will you use? _____

Group Evaluation: Use the Readers Theater Rubric to evaluate your group's performance in each area. Circle and explain your score.

Volume and Eye Contact — **Score** 1 2 3 — Explain: _____

Expression — **Score** 1 2 3 — Explain: _____

Performance — **Score** 1 2 3 — Explain: _____

Clarity — **Score** 1 2 3 — Explain: _____

What we did best: _____

What we can work on for next time: _____

Listen and Read

Description: Students listen to a recorded text while following along with the printed version.

Materials

✤ Recording device (such as a computer) and headphones

✤ Audio recordings and print versions of student texts

✤ Student directions (page 48)

✤ Listen and Read organizers (pages 49–52)

✤ Fluency Rubric (page 33)

Procedures for Teaching

1. Choose a recorded text and its print version. Model for the students how to use the technology (such as a CD player or computer), including how to play and pause (or stop) the recording.

2. Display the organizers (Before, During, After; Beginning, Middle, End; Story Elements; Favorite Part). Model previewing each organizer, then choose one to complete. Point out that for one of the organizers (Before, During, After), you need to record a prediction before listening and pause to complete the During Reading section.

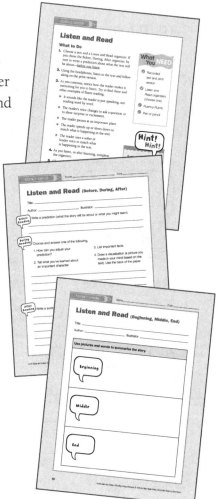

Teaching ↘ TIP

Enlarge the organizers on pages 50–52 before photocopying for students to provide more space for writing and drawing.

3. Listen to a portion of the recording and model following along on the print version. As you listen, pause to notice any of the following characteristics of fluent reading:

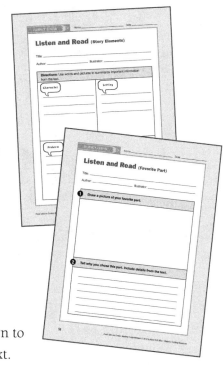

✤ It sounds like the reader is just speaking, not reading word by word.

✤ The reader's voice changes to ask a question or to show surprise or excitement.

✤ The reader pauses at an important place.

✤ The reader speeds up or slows down to match what is happening in the text.

✤ The reader uses a softer or louder voice to match what is happening in the text.

4. As you listen (or after), demonstrate how to complete the organizers.

5. After listening to the text, choose a passage to practice reading aloud, and then model using the Fluency Rubric to evaluate your reading.

Suggestions for Differentiated Learning

Provide More Support

◉ Use shorter texts, songs, or poems.

◉ Identify stopping points during the text for students to record ideas.

◉ Have students listen and follow along a second time to reinforce fluency.

Provide More Challenge

◉ Have students work in pairs or small groups and pause to discuss sections of text and/or the reader's fluency.

◉ Allow students to record stories for others to listen to. Encourage use of expression and other features of fluent reading.

Listen and Read

What to Do

1. Choose a text and a Listen and Read organizer. If you chose the Before, During, After organizer, be sure to write a prediction about what the text will be about—<u>before you listen</u>.

2. Using the headphones, listen to the text and follow along on the print version.

3. As you continue, notice how the reader makes it interesting for you to listen. Try to find these and other examples of fluent reading:

✤ It sounds like the reader is just speaking, not reading word by word.

✤ The reader's voice changes to ask a question or to show surprise or excitement.

✤ The reader pauses at an important place.

✤ The reader speeds up or slows down to match what is happening in the text.

✤ The reader uses a softer or louder voice to match what is happening in the text.

4. As you listen, or after listening, complete the organizer.

5. Choose a passage to read aloud to your teacher or a friend. First, practice reading the passage. You can listen to it again, too. Use the Fluency Rubric to evaluate your reading.

What You NEED

✓ Recorded text and print version

✓ Listen and Read organizers (choose one)

✓ Fluency Rubric

✓ Pen or pencil

Hint! Hint!

If you are using the Beginning, Middle, End organizer, stop after the first page (or section) of the text and fill in the Beginning section of the worksheet.

 Fresh Takes on Centers: Reading Comprehension © 2010 by Mary Beth Allen. Scholastic Teaching Resources

Name _____ Date _____

Listen and Read (Before, During, After)

Title: _____

Author: _____ Illustrator: _____

Before Reading Write a prediction (what the story will be about or what you might learn).

_____

_____

During Reading Answer one of the following.

➡ **How can you adjust your prediction?**

➡ **Tell what you've learned about an important character.**

➡ **List important facts.**

➡ **Draw a visualization (a picture you made in your mind based on the text). Use the back of the paper.**

_____

_____

_____

_____

After Reading Write a summary of the story or list facts about what you read.

_____

_____

_____

_____

_____

Name _____ Date _____

Listen and Read (Beginning, Middle, End)

Title: _____

Author: _____ Illustrator: _____

Use pictures and words to summarize the story.
Beginning
Middle
End

Fresh Takes on Centers: Reading Comprehension © 2010 by Mary Beth Allen. Scholastic Teaching Resources

Name _____ Date _____

Listen and Read (Story Elements)

Title: _____

Author: _____ Illustrator: _____

Directions: Use words and pictures to summarize important information from the text.

Character
_____
_____
_____

Setting
_____
_____
_____

Problem
_____
_____
_____

Solution
_____
_____
_____

Name _____ Date _____

Listen and Read (Favorite Part)

Title: _____

Author: _____ Illustrator: _____

❶ Draw a picture of your favorite part.

❷ Tell why you chose this part. Include details from the text.

_____

_____

_____

_____

_____

_____

 Fresh Takes on Centers: Reading Comprehension © 2010 by Mary Beth Allen. Scholastic Teaching Resources

Repeated Reading

Description: Students orally or silently reread a familiar text to build automaticity of words and expression.

Materials

✦ Short texts at students' independent reading levels

✦ Student directions (page 55)

✦ Fluency Rubric (page 33)

✦ Recording device (such as a computer; optional)

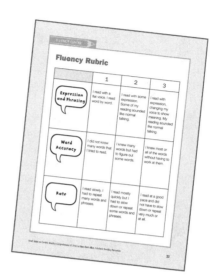

Procedures for Teaching

1. Choose a short text and model for students what fluent reading sounds like. Focus on rate, expression, attention to punctuation, and automatic reading of words. Model using the Fluency Rubric to evaluate your reading.

2. Then, read the same text again, focusing on improved expression and rate. Evaluate yourself again with the same rubric. Explain to students that when you reread a text, you are more familiar with the words and content. This makes it easier to read and understand.

3. Display another text and have students read it with you. Rate the group's reading using the Fluency Rubric. Reflect on the rate, expression, attention to punctuation, and automatic reading of the words. Discuss strategies for more fluent reading, such as scanning ahead for punctuation marks that give clues to expression. Reread the text with the class and rate again using the rubric. Reflect on areas of improvement.

4. Give pairs or small groups a text to read and rate with the rubric. Have groups discuss areas of and strategies for improvement and then repeat the exercise with the same text and rubric. Bring students together to share results as well as strategies for improving fluency.

5. Review the center materials and have students work independently to read familiar texts and rate themselves with the Fluency Rubric.

Teaching ↘ TIP

For documentation, students can record themselves reading the text.

Suggestions for Differentiated Learning

Provide More Support

- Provide an individual book box of previously read texts.

- Identify a specific component of fluency for focus. Highlight this area on the rubric for self-evaluation.

- Use poems or other short texts with a rhythmic pattern.

Provide More Challenge

- Allow students to read new, independent-level texts or slightly challenging texts.

- Have students work in small groups and rate one another's oral reading.

- Have students "buddy read" with a less able student and provide support to enhance fluency.

Repeated Reading

What to Do

1. Choose a book from your book box or choose a text that is easy for you to read.

2. Read the book (or part of it) silently, focusing on expression, pacing, and phrasing.

3. Read the book aloud to a friend.

4. Evaluate your reading using the Fluency Rubric. Have your friend evaluate you, too. Decide what you can work on to make your reading sound better.

5. Practice reading the text again, focusing on the areas you identified for improvement.

6. Evaluate your reading again using the rubric.

What You NEED

✓ A text

✓ Fluency Rubric

✓ Recording device (such as a computer)

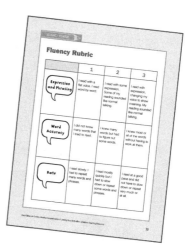

Hint! Hint!

You can use a recording device (such as a computer) to record yourself reading the book. Listen to the recording and use the Fluency Rubric to notice what you do well and what you can work on next time.

Sight Word Bingo

Description: Students work on reading the first 300 high-frequency sight words automatically.

Materials

✤ Student directions (page 58)

✤ Sight Words List (page 59)

✤ Bingo boards (pages 60–62)

✤ Sight Word Flash Cards (pages 63–66)

✤ Sight Word Flash Cards Template (page 67)

✤ Game markers

✤ Bag (or small box)

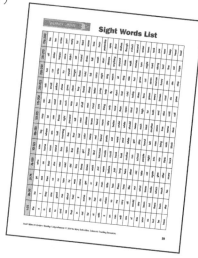

Procedures for Teaching

1. Prepare Bingo boards with a variety of sight words on them. (With help from the Sight Words List, focus on words students do not already know.) Create different versions of the Bingo board, using the same words but in different positions.

2. Prepare a flash card for each word (using the preprinted cards and the blank cards as needed). Place the cards in a bag.

3. Model playing the Bingo game. Select a Bingo flash card randomly, read the word, and look at the Bingo board to see if the word is there. If the word is there, cover it with a marker.

4. Continue the process, inviting students to help, until you fill a row and call "Bingo!"

5. Model reviewing the flash cards and the words on the Bingo board to make sure they match.

6. When students understand the process, let them try it in small groups.

7. Stock the center with sets of Bingo boards and flash cards (store these in bags) for groups of high-frequency words (25 or 30). Assign certain sets to students (for example, by placing each set in a separate box and labeling with students' names) that address words those students need to learn. For documentation, have students write the words they practiced in sentences.

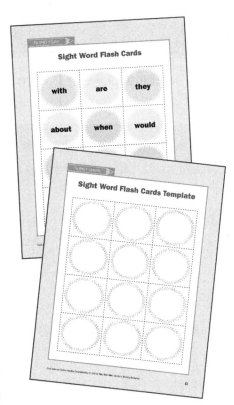

Suggestions for Differentiated Learning

Provide More Support

- Use a smaller Bingo board and fewer words.

- Include a picture or sentence on each word card.

Provide More Challenge

- Use more sophisticated vocabulary.

- Have students create their own Bingo boards, using the Sight Words List (page 59) as a resource.

Sight Word Bingo

What to Do

1. Choose a set of Bingo boards and flash cards. Each person should have a Bingo board and a set of markers.

2. Decide who will call a word first. That person takes one card from the bag and reads it aloud.

3. Players check to see if they have the word and, if so, place a marker on that space.

4. Continue, with players taking turns selecting and reading one card at a time.

5. Play until someone fills a row (horizontally, vertically, or diagonally) and calls out "Bingo!" This player reads the words that fill a row while another player checks to make sure they match.

6. Optional: Write a sentence for each word you have covered.

7. Change boards and play again.

What You NEED

✔ Bingo boards

✔ Flash cards

✔ Game markers

✔ Paper and pencils or pens (optional)

You can try a new version of Sight Word Bingo. Here are some ideas:

⇒ Play to fill all the squares around the board (top, bottom, left, and right).

⇒ Play to make an X (two diagonals).

⇒ Play to fill a board completely.

Fresh Takes on Centers: Reading Comprehension © 2010 by Mary Beth Allen. Scholastic Teaching Resources

Sight Words List

FLUENCY CENTER

1-25	26-50	51-75	76-100	101-125	126-150	151-175	176-200	201-225	226-250	251-275	276-300
the	he	go	who	saw	big	may	ran	ask	hat	off	fire
a	I	see	an	home	where	let	five	small	car	sister	ten
is	they	then	their	soon	am	use	read	yellow	write	happy	order
you	one	us	she	stand	ball	these	over	show	try	once	part
to	good	no	new	box	morning	right	such	goes	myself	didn't	early
and	me	him	said	upon	live	present	way	clean	longer	set	fat
we	about	by	did	first	four	tell	too	buy	those	round	third
that	had	was	boy	came	last	next	shall	thank	hold	dress	same
in	if	come	three	girl	color	please	own	sleep	full	fall	love
not	some	get	down	house	away	leave	most	letter	carry	wash	hear
for	up	or	work	find	red	hand	sure	jump	eight	start	yesterday
at	her	two	put	because	friend	more	thing	help	sing	always	eyes
with	do	man	were	made	pretty	why	only	fly	warm	anything	door
it	when	little	before	could	eat	better	near	don't	sit	around	clothes
on	so	has	just	book	want	under	than	fast	dog	close	though
can	my	them	long	look	year	while	open	cold	ride	walk	o'clock
will	very	how	here	mother	white	should	kind	today	hot	money	second
are	all	like	other	run	got	never	must	does	grow	turn	water
of	would	our	old	school	play	each	high	face	cut	might	town
this	any	what	take	people	found	best	far	green	seven	hard	took
your	been	know	cat	night	left	another	both	every	woman	along	pair
as	out	make	again	into	men	seem	end	brown	funny	bed	now
but	there	which	give	say	bring	tree	also	coat	yes	fine	keep
be	from	much	after	think	wish	name	until	six	ate	sat	head
have	day	his	many	back	black	dear	call	gave	stop	hope	food

Source: *The Reading Teacher's Book of Lists*, 4th ed. by E. B. Fry, Ph.D., J. E. Kress, Ed.D., and D. L. Fountoukidis, Ed.D. (Jossey-Bass, 2000)

Board 1

Sight Word
B I N G O

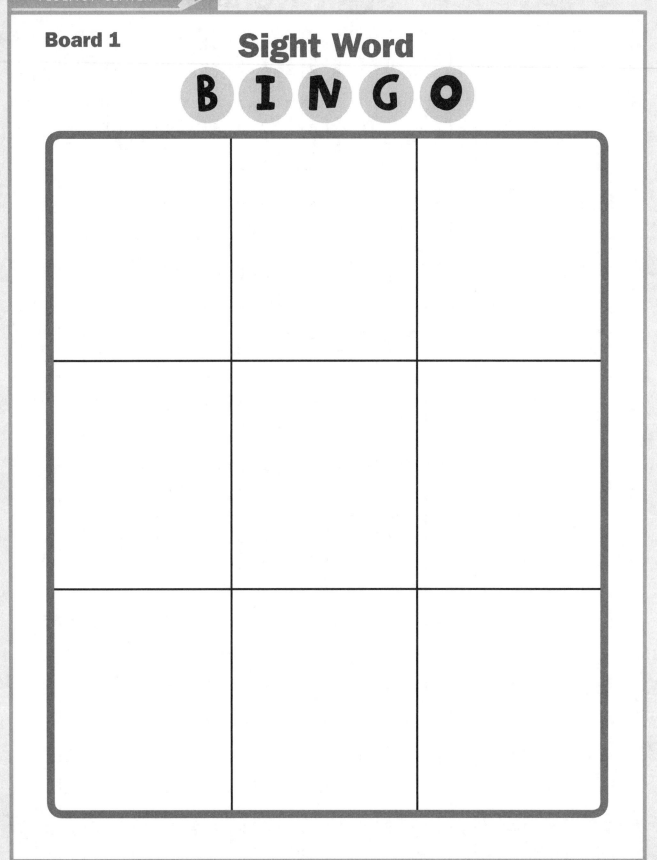

Board 2

Sight Word
BINGO

Board 3

Sight Word
BINGO

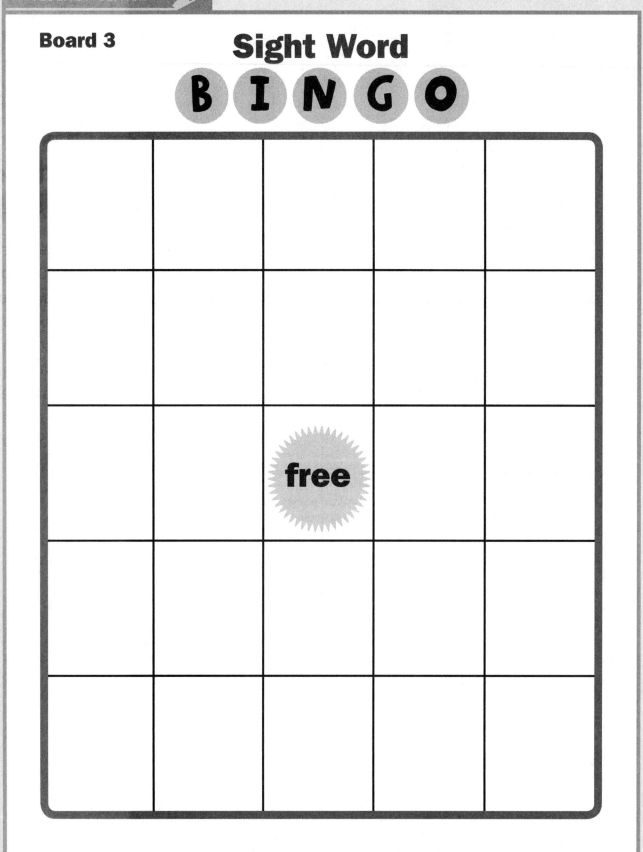

free

Fresh Takes on Centers: Reading Comprehension © 2010 by Mary Beth Allen. Scholastic Teaching Resources

Sight Word Flash Cards

with	are	they
about	when	would
there	know	which
who	before	again

Sight Word Flash Cards

saw	because	school
people	where	friend
year	use	right
next	while	another

Sight Word Flash Cards

way	sure	until
small	goes	don't
does	every	those
carry	eight	seven

Sight Word Flash Cards

once	didn't	around
close	might	early
third	hear	eyes
second	though	o'clock

Sight Word Flash Cards Template

Choral Reading

> **Description:** Students practice reading a text in pairs or small groups. They read the text together to provide peer support for fluent reading.

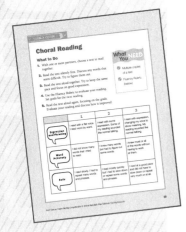

Materials

❖ Short texts (multiple copies)

❖ Chart paper (optional)

❖ Student directions (page 69)

❖ Fluency Rubric (page 33; also, bottom of page 69)

Procedures for Teaching

1. Display a short text (poem, song, chant, or paragraph) on the board or chart paper. Read it aloud first, then invite students to read it again with you. Encourage them to focus on all aspects of fluency: rate, expression, phrasing, and attention to punctuation.

2. Display and review the Fluency Rubric and have students use it to evaluate the class performance. Set goals for a repeated reading.

3. Reread the text together, focusing on the goals. Evaluate the performance again, noting progress.

4. For practice at the center, provide a variety of poems, songs, chants, and other short texts for students to read together in pairs or small groups.

Suggestions for Differentiated Learning

Provide More Support

◉ Have students listen to the text first (read it aloud for them or provide an audio recording), then read it together.

◉ Pair the struggling student with a more able student who can guide the reading.

◉ Use easier texts.

Provide More Challenge

◉ Have students work with less able students.

◉ Provide challenging texts with interesting dialogue, punctuation, or vocabulary.

Choral Reading

What to Do

1. With one or more partners, choose a text to read together.

2. Read the text silently first. Discuss any words that seem difficult. Try to figure them out.

3. Read the text aloud together. Try to keep the same pace and focus on good expression.

4. Use the Fluency Rubric to evaluate your reading. Set goals for the next reading.

5. Read the text aloud again, focusing on the goals. Evaluate your reading and discuss how it improved.

What You NEED

- ✓ Multiple copies of a text
- ✓ Fluency Rubric (below)

	1	2	3
Expression and Phrasing	I read with a flat voice. I read word by word.	I read with some expression. Some of my reading sounded like normal talking.	I read with expression, changing my voice to show meaning. My reading sounded like normal talking.
Word Accuracy	I did not know many words that I tried to read.	I knew many words but had to figure out some words.	I knew most or all of the words without having to work at them.
Rate	I read slowly. I had to repeat many words and phrases.	I read mostly quickly but I had to slow down or repeat some words and phrases.	I read at a good pace and did not have to slow down or repeat very much or at all.

Recorded Reading

Description: Students record themselves reading a new text, score it with a rubric, and set a goal for improving fluency. They repeat the process and reflect on progress.

Materials

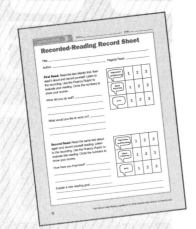

+ Student texts

+ Recording device (such as a computer)

+ Student directions (page 71)

+ Fluency Rubric (page 33; also, bottom of page 71)

+ Recorded-Reading Record Sheet (page 72)

Procedures for Teaching

1. Model the process of getting ready to read a text aloud and record yourself. Review procedures for operating the recording device.

2. Record yourself reading the text. After, listen to the recording and use the Fluency Rubric to evaluate fluency, circling a score for each category. Use your score to set a fluency goal—for example, to improve the reading rate, expression, or phrasing. Record your rubric scores and a goal on the record sheet. (You may intentionally read in such a way to demonstrate an area for improvement. Then discuss how to make it better.)

3. Read and record the text again, focusing on the goal. Evaluate the reading again with the rubric. Think aloud about your improvement and record this on the record sheet.

4. Have students practice this process individually, in pairs, or in small groups.

5. For independent work at the center, provide a variety of leveled texts to accommodate all students. Have students repeat the process of recording and evaluating themselves.

Suggestions for Differentiated Learning

Provide More Support

- Use shorter texts or poems.

- Adjust the rubric to focus on one or two aspects of fluency.

Provide More Challenge

- Provide more complex texts.

- Allow students to work in pairs and evaluate each other.

Recorded Reading

What to Do

1. Choose a text to read. Read it silently first.

2. Read and record the text.

3. Listen to your recorded reading and evaluate yourself using the Fluency Rubric. Decide what you did well and what you would like to do better. Write your goal on the record sheet.

4. Practice reading the text again, focusing on your goal.

5. Read and record the text again. Use the Fluency Rubric to evaluate this reading. Complete the record sheet to tell how you improved your reading.

What You NEED

- ✓ Student texts
- ✓ Recording device (such as a computer)
- ✓ Fluency Rubric (below)
- ✓ Recorded-Reading Record Sheet

	1	2	3
Expression and Phrasing	I read with a flat voice. I read word by word.	I read with some expression. Some of my reading sounded like normal talking.	I read with expression, changing my voice to show meaning. My reading sounded like normal talking.
Word Accuracy	I did not know many words that I tried to read.	I knew many words but had to figure out some words.	I knew most or all of the words without having to work at them.
Rate	I read slowly. I had to repeat many words and phrases.	I read mostly quickly but I had to slow down or repeat some words and phrases.	I read at a good pace and did not have to slow down or repeat very much or at all.

Name _____   Date _____

Recorded-Reading Record Sheet

Title: _____

Author: _____   Page(s) Read: _____

First Read: Read the text silently first, then read it aloud and record yourself. Listen to the recording. Use the Fluency Rubric to evaluate your reading. Circle the numbers to show your scores.

What did you do well? _____

_____

_____

What would you like to work on? _____

_____

_____

Expression and Phrasing	1	2	3
Word Accuracy	1	2	3
Rate	1	2	3

Second Read: Read the same text aloud again and record yourself reading. Listen to the recording. Use the Fluency Rubric to evaluate this reading. Circle the numbers to show your scores.

How have you improved? _____

_____

_____

Explain a new reading goal. _____

_____

_____

Expression and Phrasing	1	2	3
Word Accuracy	1	2	3
Rate	1	2	3

Fresh Takes on Centers: Reading Comprehension © 2010 by Mary Beth Allen. Scholastic Teaching Resources

Partner Reading

Description: Students work with a partner to practice reading a text with greater fluency. The partner provides scaffolding with rate or unknown words, as needed.

Materials

✤ Student texts (books, poems, short stories, articles)

✤ Recording device (such as a computer; optional)

✤ Student directions (page 74)

✤ Fluency Rubric (page 33; also, bottom of page 74)

Procedures for Teaching

1. Choose a text to read aloud to the class and select another adult or student to be your partner. Explain the process of partner reading and model how to do it. Begin by using sticky notes to mark passages for you and your partner to read. Then take turns as you read aloud the text. Show how while one of you is reading, the other is following along and listening. Have the person who is listening model appropriate ways of helping—for example, by identifying a challenging word or helping with punctuation.

2. Provide a short text for students to practice partner reading. (Students can read the text silently first.)Encourage students to support each other, as needed. (It is helpful to pair a more able reader with a less able reader.)

3. To prepare the center for independent work, include books and other texts that have previously been read aloud to the class (books, poems, short stories, and articles).

> **Teaching → TIP**
>
> **Optional:** Students can record themselves reading as a way to document fluency. They can score one another using the Fluency Rubric.

Suggestions for Differentiated Learning

Provide More Support

◉ Use only independent-level texts.

◉ Partner students with a more able reader.

◉ Preview new vocabulary

Provide More Challenge

◉ Use more challenging texts.

◉ Have students work with and support less skilled readers.

◉ Include short historic speeches and other content-related texts for students to read aloud.

Partner Reading

What to Do

1. Choose a familiar text. Use sticky notes to section the text into the passages you and your partner will each read.

2. Decide who will go first. That partner then begins reading aloud. The other partner follows along and listens, giving help, if needed.

3. After the first reader finishes reading, the partners switch roles and continue with the next passage.

4. Continue reading and helping until you have finished the text.

5. Optional: Evaluate your reading using the Fluency Rubric.

What You NEED

- ✓ A text (book, poem, short story, or article)
- ✓ Sticky notes
- ✓ Recording device (such as a computer; optional)
- ✓ Fluency Rubric (below; optional)

	1	2	3
Expression and Phrasing	I read with a flat voice. I read word by word.	I read with some expression. Some of my reading sounded like normal talking.	I read with expression, changing my voice to show meaning. My reading sounded like normal talking.
Word Accuracy	I did not know many words that I tried to read.	I knew many words but had to figure out some words.	I knew most or all of the words without having to work at them.
Rate	I read slowly. I had to repeat many words and phrases.	I read mostly quickly but I had to slow down or repeat some words and phrases.	I read at a good pace and did not have to slow down or repeat very much or at all.

 Fresh Takes on Centers: Reading Comprehension © 2010 by Mary Beth Allen. Scholastic Teaching Resources

Setting Up an Independent Reading Center

The purpose of this center is to allow students the opportunity to read many texts on their own. This is a time to practice all of the skills and strategies that have been taught in read-aloud and guided settings. Students will spend most of the time reading and some time documenting the thinking they use while reading.

Students can read from a variety of genres and on an assortment of topics. (See Suggested Genres, page 77.) Students should have some choice as to what they read, but this can be a scaffolded choice. For example, it is helpful to have texts relate to topics you are studying in other aspects of the curriculum. If you are implementing a literature study on a particular genre, such as mystery books, then you would want to have an assortment of mystery books, at varying levels, for students to read. If you are studying the American Revolution, then offer a variety of books—fiction, nonfiction, poetry, biography, and so on—related to this topic. This approach encourages students to make important connections at the center to what they are studying in other areas. They will be able to read more successfully because they will have some background knowledge, while at the same time they will broaden their knowledge about the topic with the further reading provided at the center. Students can then also share information and ideas from their work at the Independent Reading Center during the content area time, furthering the connections they make—and building their confidence as readers and as learners.

A Note About Documentation

Although most educators agree that the only way to get better at reading is to do more reading, there is some debate about what children are actually doing during independent reading (NICHHD, 2000). Therefore, it is critical that we have students apply what we have taught them and that we build in ways to hold them accountable while reading independently. To that end, we want to teach, and have students use, processes to document their thinking at some point during the reading. That way we can know if they are actually reading the text and are engaged in thinking before, during, and after reading. The caution is to not require so much documentation or such superficial documentation that students lose both interest in and enjoyment of the reading. The activities at this center are designed with this in mind and offer enjoyable yet informative ways to guide students in documenting their thinking.

Teaching TIP

This center can be set up and in use throughout the entire year with minimal changes. You can change the literature, the products, or the process. Consider using themes at the center to keep interest high. A few options are Mystery, Biography, Informational Texts (related to Content-area topics), Author Studies, and Poetry. Invite students to suggest themes of interest as well.

Connections to the Standards

The center activities in this section support the following standards for students in grades 3–5, outlined by Mid-continent Research for Education and Learning (McREL), an organization that collects and synthesizes national and state K–12 curriculum standards.

Reading

Uses the general skills and strategies of the reading process

- Previews text, for example, by skimming and using text format
- Establishes a purpose for reading
- Makes, confirms, and revises simple predictions about what will be found in a text
- Uses phonetic and structural analysis techniques, syntactic structure, and semantic context to decode unknown words
- Uses a variety of context clues to decode unknown words
- Uses word reference materials, such as a dictionary or thesaurus, to understand unknown words
- Understands level-appropriate reading vocabulary
- Monitors own reading strategies and makes modifications as needed
- Adjusts speed of reading to suit purpose and difficulty of the material
- Understands the author's purpose or point of view
- Uses personal criteria, such as interest or text difficulty, to select reading material

Uses reading skills and strategies to understand and interpret a variety of literary texts

- Understands ways in which language, such as alliteration, hyperbole, and rhythm, is used in literary texts
- Knows the defining characteristics of a variety of literary forms and genres
- Understands the basic concept of plot
- Understands similarities and differences within and among literary works from various genre and cultures
- Understands elements of character development
- Knows themes that recur across literary works
- Understands the ways in which language is used in literary texts
- Makes connections between characters or simple events in a literary work and people or events in his or her own life

Uses reading skills and strategies to understand and interpret a variety of informational texts

- Uses reading skills and strategies to understand informational texts
- Knows defining characteristics of textbooks and other informational texts
- Uses features of nonfiction such as table of contents, headings, visual aids, glossary, and index to locate information
- Summarizes and paraphrases information
- Uses prior knowledge and experience to understand and respond to new information

Source: *Content Knowledge: A Compendium of Standards and Benchmarks for K–12 Education* (4th ed.). Mid-continent Research for Education and Learning, 2004 (http://www.mcrel.org/standards–benchmarks).

Suggested Genres

✤ Biography (texts about people, including informational and fictional accounts of their lives)

✤ Fairy Tales and Folktales

✤ Fantasy

✤ Historical Fiction (fictional text that is based on historical facts)

✤ Informational Text (from Social Studies and Science areas of study)

✤ Modern Fiction (fiction that deals with contemporary issues that children and adolescents face in day-to-day living)

✤ Mystery

✤ Poetry (individual poems or collections of poems)

✤ Science Fiction (fiction that portrays life in the future or in other worlds)

Independent Reading Center Materials

✤ Lots of books in varied genres and levels

✤ Audio books

✤ Independent Reading Center Self-Assessment (page 80)

✤ Student activity pages

✤ Samples of completed activities

✤ Sticky notes

✤ Journals

✤ Examples of excellent work

Teaching the Process

Students of all ages should read independently every day. It is important to build in time for children to read for pleasure, and it is critical that you teach children how to document their thinking so they can share ideas later. Use read-aloud time to model fluent and expressive reading as well as processes for documenting thinking before, during, and after reading. You can teach students how to do this by using a direct instruction process of explaining, demonstrating, guiding, and practicing. The following procedure works quite well to ensure that all students can find success in documenting their thinking during independent reading.

1. Choose a book to read aloud to students. In advance of reading, select one of the formats in this section for documenting your thinking—for example, "I Wonder" Organizers (page 95). Make sure the format you select is suited to the strategy you are demonstrating and the text you are reading.

Teaching ↘ TIP

As you prepare to introduce a center activity, preview the lesson (Procedures for Teaching) to determine the amount of time you will need to spend on the material. Many activities are best taught over a period of several days.

2. While reading aloud, demonstrate the thinking you are doing as you read. This can focus on one or more of the strategies readers use *before reading* (activating prior knowledge, making connections, asking questions, making predictions, making inferences, setting purposes), *during reading* (making connections, creating images, revising predictions, answering questions, asking more questions, summarizing, and synthesizing), and *after reading* (answering questions, summarizing). Model using one of the Independent Reading Center activity sheets to record this thinking so you can share it with others.

3. Use the next part of the same book or text, or choose another, to engage students in using the strategy. Guide them by posing prompts and questions to scaffold their thinking related to the strategy you are targeting. Encourage students to share ideas with partners or in small groups and then with the class. Continue to model using the activity sheet to document thinking as students share their own thinking. Have students document their ideas as well to provide practice in recording their thinking while they read. Gradually reduce the amount of support as students show they understand the thinking and the process.

4. Once students have demonstrated the ability to apply the strategy and express their thinking orally and to document their thinking through writing and drawing, encourage individuals, pairs, or small groups to read or listen to a text, and apply the strategy and record their thinking.

5. Share the Independent Reading Center Self-Assessment and explain how to complete it. While you may not require that students complete the assessment each time they visit the center, it is a helpful tool for periodically (such as weekly) monitoring students' work and assessing understanding of comprehension strategies.

6. When you think students are ready, place the same activity at the center for use during independent reading time.

7. Continue modeling new activity sheets in this way as you prepare to add them to the center.

This process should be completed during the mini-lesson phase of a Readers Workshop, or during the read-aloud portion of guided comprehension. It serves two purposes: First, it is the time for direct instruction of the comprehension strategies and the processes for documenting thinking; second, it provides a time to instruct students so they can learn to apply the thinking and the documenting on their own. There are many points to check for understanding, so you know whether you should place the activity at the center or reteach it so students can become more competent users of the strategy and the documentation.

Throughout this process, observe students to determine if they need more or less support. If students seem to be able to apply the strategies and document their thinking successfully, then they are ready to work independently at the center. If students are not ready to participate independently, then continue to demonstrate and provide guidance. Use this process as a guide for introducing new activities at the center and to teach and revisit comprehension strategies on an ongoing basis. With the appropriate support or challenge, all students can use comprehension strategies and document their thinking using a variety of topics and formats.

Adapting the Process

Some students will need more support in applying the comprehension strategies and documenting their thinking. Others will be ready for more of a challenge. The following suggestions will allow all students to participate successfully.

Suggestions for Differentiated Learning

Provide More Support

- Provide an adapted version of the activity sheets for documenting thinking. Allow more space for writing, decrease the number of answers, and offer hints.

- Read and record the texts for use at the center. Allow students to listen and follow along, and then record their thinking.

- Allow drawing and labeling as an alternative to writing.

- Scribe as students dictate responses.

- Allow students to work with a more skilled partner.

- Highlight portions of activity sheets for students to complete.

- Choose texts that provide obvious opportunities for applying the comprehension strategy.

Provide More Challenge

- Allow students to use open-ended journals to record their thinking before, during, and after reading.

- Give students choices as to how they will record their thinking.

- Encourage the use of more than one strategy for applying and documenting.

- Choose more complex texts to challenge critical thinking.

- Have students share ideas in book clubs or literature circles.

Name _____ Date _____

Independent Reading Center
Self-Assessment

	Basic	Good	Great
I chose a book that was the right level for me.			
I documented my thinking… Before Reading			
I documented my thinking… During Reading			
I documented my thinking… After Reading			
I used thinking beyond the text.			

While working at this center, I used the following strategies:

_____

_____

_____

I learned: _____

_____

Next time I would like to try: _____

_____

Fresh Takes on Centers: Reading Comprehension © 2010 by Mary Beth Allen. Scholastic Teaching Resources

Acrostic Summaries

Description: Students use the letters in a key word to write summaries or character analyses.

Materials

✦ Familiar student texts

✦ Student directions (page 83)

✦ Acrostic forms (pages 84–85)

✦ Thesaurus and dictionary

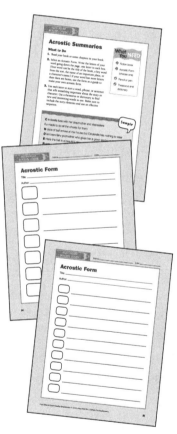

Procedures for Teaching

1. Show students the format for writing acrostics and share one or more completed examples. (See page 82.) Explain that these acrostics can be retellings of a chapter or story, or may describe characters. If retelling a story or chapter, discuss how the acrostic includes story elements and uses an effective sequence.

2. Select a familiar story or character and demonstrate the process for creating an acrostic, thinking aloud about the choices as you write the acrostic on the board or another visual display. This is a good time to model using a thesaurus or dictionary to find new and interesting words to use.

3. Guide students to create an acrostic as a class using a familiar character or story. You might begin with favorite picture books to simplify the process at first. Invite volunteers to use a thesaurus and dictionary to replace some words with stronger choices.

4. Review the materials at the center. Have students work at the center to create individual or group acrostics related to the stories they are reading.

Suggestions for Differentiated Learning

Provide More Support

- Elicit language from students and scribe for them.

- Have students complete a partially filled-in acrostic.

- Provide sentence or phrase starters.

- Encourage students to use words and short phrases.

- Provide a word bank or list of ideas as applicable.

Provide More Challenge

- Have students use a wrapping technique, allowing one line to wrap into the next.

- Make each line a trait about a character in a story or a famous person.

- Make each line a complete sentence.

- Encourage students to consult references to use more vivid language.

- Make the entire acrostic one complete sentence or idea.

Retelling Acrostic

Based on *Crickwing* by Janell Cannon (Harcourt, 2000)

C ockroach lives deep in the forest and likes to make art from his food

R etreats to safe place when larger animals steal his food

I rritated by this and decides to pick on the leaf-cutting ants

C reates dastardly ideas to bully the ants

K ept interfering with the leaf-cutting ant's work

W anted by the queen ant for slowing supply of food

I s caught by the ants but they feel bad and let him go

N eeds to make up to ants so creates sculpted anteater to scare army ants

G ets to stay with the ants and be their chef

Character Analysis Acrostic

Based on *Olivia* by Ian Falconer (Atheneum, 2000)

O n the go with her mother and brother Ian

L ikes to get her way

I s very active

V ery picky about the clothes she wears

I nterested in the arts—music, art, dance

A good negotiator, especially at bedtime

Acrostic Summaries

What to Do

1. Read your book or some chapters in your book.

2. Select an Acrostic Form. Write the letters of your word going down the page, one letter in each box. (Your word can be the title of the book, a key word from the text, the name of an important place, or a character's name.) If your word has more letters than there are boxes, use the form as a guide to make your own acrostic form.

3. Use each letter to start a word, phrase, or sentence that tells something important about the story or character. Use a thesaurus or dictionary to find new and interesting words to use. Make sure to include the story elements and use an effective sequence.

What You NEED

- ✓ Fiction book
- ✓ Acrostic Form (choose one)
- ✓ Pencil or pen
- ✓ Thesaurus and dictionary

Sample

C inderella lives with her stepmother and stepsisters

I s made to do all the chores for them

N otice of ball arrives at the house but Cinderella has nothing to wear

D iscovers fairy godmother who gives her a gown and a carriage

E nters the ball in a beautiful dress

R eels around the dance floor with the prince

E xits the ball in a hurry at midnight and leaves a glass slipper behind

L onely prince tries to find the owner of the glass slipper

L ets the glass slipper slide onto Cinderella's foot

A nd the couple lives happily ever after

Name _____ Date _____

Acrostic Form

Title: _____

Author: _____

Name _____ Date _____

Acrostic Form

Title: _____

Author: _____

 _____

_____

_____

_____

_____

_____

_____

_____

_____

_____

During-Reading Bookmarks

Description: Students use a set of bookmarks to record their thinking while reading a text. Bookmarks can be labeled with types of thinking or can be blank for students to decide.

Materials

✦ Student texts

✦ Student directions (page 88)

✦ Bookmark templates (pages 89–90)

Procedures for Teaching

1. Choose a text and a bookmark template. Cut out the bookmark, then model the process for using the bookmark to document thinking. Read a section of text aloud and record your thinking on the bookmark.

Try to demonstrate an example for each type of bookmark students will be using (Connections, Predictions, Important Information, Inferences, Interesting Words or Phrases, Sensory Images, Need to Clarify, Questions). Explain your thinking for each.

2. Read another section of text aloud and use guiding questions to help students record their thinking on a bookmark. Move about the room and guide or prompt, as needed. Allow students to share ideas with a partner, small group, or the class.

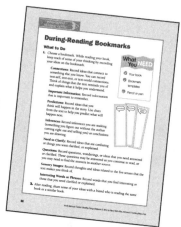

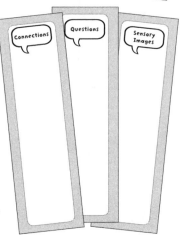

3. Read another section of text aloud and have the students record their thinking on another bookmark. Provide additional assistance, if necessary. Encourage children to share and explain their thinking with a partner, small group, or the class.

4. Have individuals, pairs, or small groups read a text and record thinking on several different bookmarks. Use this to determine whether students are ready to try this independently at the center.

5. Stock the center with bookmarks (cut them out in advance). Have students use the bookmarks to keep track of their thinking while reading books they choose or for assigned reading for other subject areas. They can use their bookmarks as a resource to discuss the text or to demonstrate their understandings.

Suggestions for Differentiated Learning

Provide More Support

- Section the text and provide key words or prompts for documenting ideas.

- Allow students to sketch and label their thinking.

- Take students' language and scribe the thinking.

- Provide students with the bookmark that is best suited to their needs or text.

Provide More Challenge

- Have students record ideas to defend their thinking.

- Let students section the text on their own and record thinking accordingly.

- Have students use more than one bookmark with a text.

- Provide other categories for documenting thinking, such as Beginnings or Endings.

During-Reading Bookmarks

What to Do

1. Choose a bookmark. While reading your book, keep track of some of your thinking by recording your ideas on the bookmark.

Connections: Record ideas that connect to something else you know. You can record text-self, text-text, or text-world connections. Think of things that the text reminds you of and explain what it helps you understand.

Important Information: Record information that is important to remember.

Predictions: Record what you think will happen in the story. Use clues from the text to help you predict what will happen next.

Inferences: Record inferences you are making (something you figure out without the author coming right out and telling you) or conclusions you are drawing.

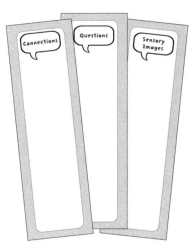

Need to Clarify: Record ideas that are confusing or things you want clarified, or explained.

Questions: Record questions, wonderings, or ideas that you need answered or clarified. These questions may be answered as you continue to read, or you may need to find the answers in another source.

Sensory Images: Record thoughts and ideas related to the five senses that the text makes you think of.

Interesting Words or Phrases: Record words that you find interesting or those that you need clarified or explained.

2. After reading, share some of your ideas with a friend who is reading the same book or a similar book.

Fresh Takes on Centers: Reading Comprehension © 2010 by Mary Beth Allen. Scholastic Teaching Resources

Bookmark Templates

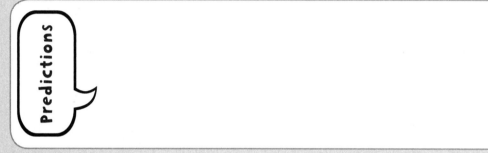

Bookmark Templates

Interesting Words or Phrases

Sensory Images

Questions

Need to Clarify

Fresh Takes on Centers: Reading Comprehension © 2010 by Mary Beth Allen. Scholastic Teaching Resources

After-Reading Book Jackets

Description: After reading, students use information about the text, the author, and the illustrator to create a new jacket for the book.

Materials

✤ Student texts

✤ Student directions (page 93)

✤ Book Jacket Template (page 94; enlarge)

✤ Pencil or pen, markers, other art supplies

Procedures for Teaching

1. After reading a text, explain to students that you are now going to use ideas about the text and the author (and illustrator) to create a new jacket for the book.

2. Model the process of thinking about the information, gathering the information, and recording the information on the book jacket template. Model each part of the process, displaying the book jacket for students to see.

✤ **Cover:** Design a new cover for the book. Make sure the illustration captures the theme or important ideas from the text.

✤ **Front Inside Panel:** Write a short summary of the book, including important information but not giving away the ending.

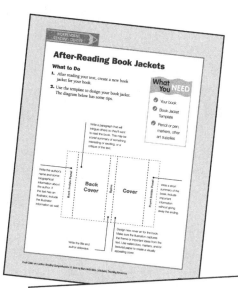

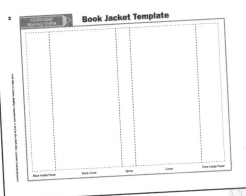

Teaching TIP

Enlarge the Book Jacket Template to provide students with more space for writing and drawing.

✤ **Spine:** Write the title and author sideways.

✤ **Back Cover:** Write a paragraph that will intrigue others and encourage them to read the book. This may be a brief summary of something interesting or exciting, or a critique of the text.

✤ **Back Inside Panel:** Write the author's name and some biographical information about the author. If the text has an illustrator, include the illustrator information as well.

3. Invite students to help with any part of the process—for example, let a volunteer draw a new illustration for the cover.

4. Guide students to follow the same process to create book jackets for a familiar book. Students may work in pairs or small groups to complete the process.

5. When students demonstrate they know how to create book jackets that capture the main ideas of the text, make this a choice at the center and encourage them to make additional jackets after reading other texts.

Suggestions for Differentiated Learning

Provide More Support

- Provide a paragraph frame for each section and have students fill in the information.
- Have students organize information on a separate sheet of paper before creating the book jacket.
- Display sample book jackets from published books to provide students with models.

Provide More Challenge

- Have students review the inside flap and back cover copy from published books and practice writing in the same style.
- Suggest students compare book jackets for variations in the format and use them as a guide for creating their own version.
- Have students use a dictionary or thesaurus to hone word choice. (You might discuss the idea of a book jacket being like "advertising" for a book and the importance of word choice in that regard.)

After-Reading Book Jackets

What to Do

1. After reading your text, create a new book jacket for your book.

2. Use the template to design your book jacket. The diagram below has some tips.

What You NEED

- ✓ Your book
- ✓ Book Jacket Template
- ✓ Pencil or pen, markers, other art supplies

Write a paragraph that will intrigue others so they'll want to read the book. This may be a brief summary of something interesting or exciting, or a critique of the text.

Write the author's name and some biographical information about the author. If the text has an illustrator, include the illustrator information as well.

Back Inside Panel

Back Cover

Spine

Cover

Front Inside Panel

Write a short summary of the book. Include important information without giving away the ending.

Design new cover art for the book. Make sure the illustration captures the theme or important ideas from the text. Use watercolors, markers, and/or textured paper to create a visually appealing cover.

Write the title and author sideways.

Book Jacket Template

Front Inside Panel

Cover

Spine

Back Cover

Back Inside Panel

Fresh Takes on Centers: Reading Comprehension © 2010 by Mary Beth Allen. Scholastic Teaching Resources

"I Wonder" Organizers

Description: This process actively engages students in thinking while reading, using "I wonder" statements to question the text and make predictions.

Materials

✦ Student texts

✦ Student directions (page 97)

✦ "I Wonder" Chart and Bookmark Template (pages 98–99)

✦ Large sticky notes

Procedures for Teaching

1. Choose a format for sharing "I wondering" statements:

   ✦ "I Wonder" Chart

   ✦ "I Wonder" Bookmark

   ✦ Sticky Note Wonderings (To make these, write the words "I Wonder: _____" at the top of the sticky notes and "What I Found: _____" at the bottom.)

2. Explain to students what a "wondering" is and how we use this sort of questioning in everyday life. Wonder aloud about the weather, a visitor, or an expectation for later in the day, beginning each sentence with "I wonder." Then connect this to what readers do before and during reading, using clues in the text to wonder about something or make a prediction.

3. Use a read-aloud to model the activity. Display the cover of a book and wonder aloud about the title, the cover illustrations, and the back cover. Explain what prompted each "wondering." Model how to share

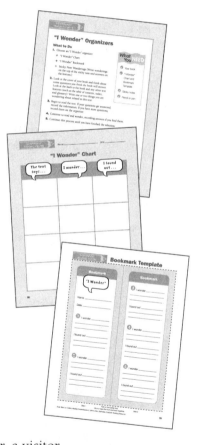

or document your "wonderings," verbally stating them or recording them on one of the organizers. Read the first section of the text and continue to model the strategy, orally and in writing. If your questions get answered in the text, record that information.

4. Read another section of text and guide students to generate their own wonderings, including questions they have and predictions they are making. Use prompts such as "The text said… Does that make you wonder about something?" or "The character did… What does that make you wonder about?" Use a Think-Pair-Share session to have students share and discuss the things they "wonder" about.

5. When the students appear to be able to generate meaningful wonderings, read aloud another section of text and have them verbally share or document what they wonder about in writing. Share some with the class and have students explain their thinking.

6. When students demonstrate they can use the "I Wonder" organizers effectively, encourage them to use these organizers to document their thinking during independent reading.

Suggestions for Differentiated Learning

Provide More Support

- Read small sections of text and provide prompts to generate wonderings.

- Use large sticky notes to flag specific pages or sections for students to read. Write "I Wonder: _____" at the top of the sticky notes and "What I Found: _____" at the bottom.

- Choose texts that are easy to read but have more complex concepts to allow for natural "wondering" opportunities.

Provide More Challenge

- Allow students to select their own stopping points to generate wonderings.

- Encourage students to write any information they find related to what they wonder on a separate section of the organizer.

- Have students list the text clues that sparked their wonderings.

- Have students use their "wonderings" to write a paragraph about what they read.

"I Wonder" Organizers

What to Do

1. Choose an "I Wonder" organizer:

✚ "I Wonder" Chart

✚ "I Wonder" Bookmark

✚ Sticky Note Wonderings (Write wonderings on the top of the sticky note and answers on the bottom.)

2. Look at the cover of your book and think about some questions you think the book will answer. Look at the back to the book and any other text features (such as the table of contents, index, and glossary). Write one or two things you are wondering about related to this text.

3. Begin to read the text. If your questions get answered, record the information. If you have more questions, record them on the organizer.

4. Continue to read and wonder, recording answers if you find them.

5. Continue this process until you have finished the selection.

What You NEED

✓ Your book

✓ "I Wonder" Chart and Bookmark Template

✓ Sticky notes

✓ Pencil or pen

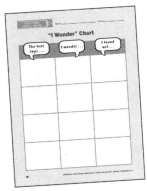

"I Wonder" Chart

"I Wonder" Bookmark

What I wonder:

What I found:

Sticky Note Wonderings

Name _____ Date _____

"I Wonder" Chart

The text says...	I wonder...	I found out...

Bookmark Template

Bookmark

"I Wonder"

Name _____

Date _____

1 I wonder _____
_____
_____ .

I found out _____
_____
_____ .

2 I wonder _____
_____
_____ .

I found out _____
_____
_____ .

Bookmark

3 I wonder _____
_____
_____ .

I found out _____
_____
_____ .

4 I wonder _____
_____
_____ .

I found out _____
_____
_____ .

5 I wonder _____
_____
_____ .

I found out _____
_____
_____ .

Side 1

Fold on the center line.
Glue or tape the front and back together.

Side 2

Thought Bubble Organizers

Description: Students use a series of sketches and words to document a character's thinking.

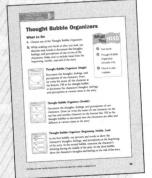

Materials

✤ Student texts

✤ Student directions (page 101)

✤ Thought Bubble Organizers (pages 102–104)

Procedures for Teaching

1. Choose a text to read aloud. During or after the read-aloud, pause to demonstrate how to use one of the Thought Bubble Organizers (Single, Double, or Beginning, Middle, End) to document a character's thoughts, feelings, and perceptions. Include sketches, labels, and phrases as documentation of your thinking.

2. Read another section of text or a different text and guide students to complete their own Thought Bubble Organizer of the character. Use guiding questions and prompts, as needed. Gradually reduce the amount of prompting as students show they understand the process. Allow students to share ideas with a partner, a small group, or the class.

3. Read another section of text or a different text and have students document the character's thoughts, feelings, and perceptions using another copy of the Thought Bubble Organizer. Use this to determine if children are ready to use the Thought Bubble Organizers at the center after reading a text or chapters of a novel.

Suggestions for Differentiated Learning

Provide More Support

- Read the text in small sections and have students record the character's thoughts.

- Choose texts that have very clear characters and very explicit thinking.

- Use a computer and clip art as a way to represent a character's thoughts, ideas, or perceptions.

Provide More Challenge

- Choose texts with more complex characters.

- Have students sketch two characters' thoughts, feelings, and perceptions as a way to compare and contrast the two.

- Have students sketch a character's thoughts, feelings, and perceptions for each chapter or section of book and then analyze how the character has changed over time.

Thought Bubble Organizers

What to Do

1. Choose one of the Thought Bubble Organizers.

2. While reading your book or after you read, use sketches and words to document the thoughts, feelings, and perceptions of one or two of the characters. Make sure to include ideas from the beginning, middle, and end of the story.

What You NEED

✓ Your book

✓ Thought Bubble Organizers (choose one)

✓ Pencil or pen, markers

Thought Bubble Organizer (Single)

Document the thoughts, feelings, and perceptions of one character. Draw (or write the name of) the character at the bottom. Fill in the thought bubble to document the character's thoughts, feelings, and perceptions at various times in the story.

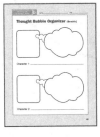

Thought Bubble Organizer (Double)

Document the thoughts, feelings, and perceptions of two characters. Draw (or write the name of) one character on the top line and another character on the bottom line. Fill in the thought bubbles to document how the characters are alike and different at various times in the story.

Thought Bubble Organizer (Beginning, Middle, End)

In the first bubble, use pictures and words to show the character's thoughts, feelings, and perceptions at the beginning of the story. In the second bubble, represent the character's thinking during the middle of the story. In the third bubble, show the character's thoughts and feelings at the end of the story.

Name _____ Date _____

Thought Bubble Organizer (Single)

Text: _____

Character: _____

Name _____   Date _____

Thought Bubble Organizer (Double)

Character 1: _____

Character 2: _____

Thought Bubble Organizer

(Beginning, Middle, End)

Beginning Character: _____

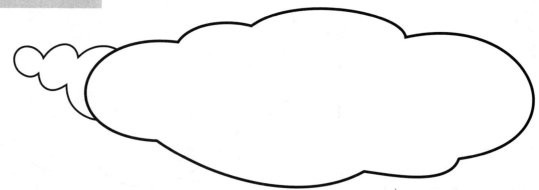

Middle Character: _____

End Character: _____

Fresh Takes on Centers: Reading Comprehension © 2010 by Mary Beth Allen. Scholastic Teaching Resources

"Say Something"

Description: Students read a text in small segments and share ideas with a partner or a group to make a connection, clarify, summarize, or extend understanding.

Materials

✤ Student texts (multiple copies)

✤ Student directions (page 107)

✤ "Say Something" Organizers (pages 108–109)

✤ "Say Something" Record Sheets (pages 110–111)

Procedures for Teaching

1. Choose a read-aloud to model the activity. Select a portion of text to read and mark the end place with a sticky note.

2. During reading, pause to think aloud about a connection you made (or something you want to clarify, summarize, or extend). Model using one of the "Say Something" Organizers for help as you think about the text. (These organizers prompt students to ask questions, make predictions, make connections, explain sensory images, cite important facts, and make inferences.) Then model using one of the "Say Something" Record Sheets to document your thinking. Read aloud what you wrote to a partner.

3. Read on in the selection and continue to model the process, first thinking aloud about the text, recording your thinking, then saying it aloud to a partner. Repeat this process until students understand.

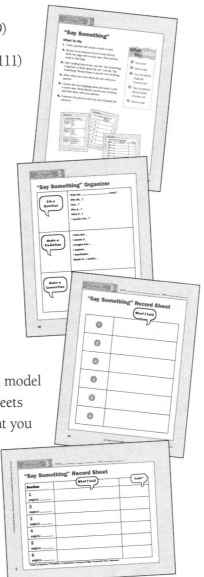

Teaching ⭨ TIP

Students can also keep track of their ideas on sticky notes or in journals.

4. Provide pairs of students with organizers and record sheets and have them practice the process as you continue reading to predetermined stopping points. Have students think of something to say related to the text, write it on the record sheet, and then say it to their partner. Use guiding questions as needed, such as "Does this make you want to know more? Does it make you wonder about anything? Are you making any connections to the character or the actions?"

5. Continue to read aloud to predetermined stopping points, gradually reducing the amount of prompting as students show they understand. Have students think, record, and then say something to their partner. Monitor their understanding, and guide as necessary.

6. When students have demonstrated they understand the process, add this during-reading activity as an option at the center.

Suggestions for Differentiated Learning

Provide More Support

- Read small sections of text and use specific guiding questions.

- Put pages and guiding questions on the organizer so students can manage independently.

- Help students choose texts that they will be able to say something meaningful about.

Provide More Challenge

- Allow students to select their own stopping points.

- Encourage students to write and say an explanation about their thinking.

- Have students generate their own ideas for what to say that helps them understand the characters or text. Students can also create their own codes for the types of thinking they are using.

"Say Something"

What to Do

1. Find a partner and choose a book to read.

2. Decide on an amount of text to read silently. Mark the page with a sticky note. Each partner reads to that page.

3. After reading that section, use the "Say Something" Organizer to think about the text. Use the "Say Something" Record Sheet to record your thinking.

4. Share what you wrote about the text with your partner.

5. Choose the next stopping point and mark it with a sticky note. Read silently, record your thinking, and then share with your partner.

6. Continue this process until you have finished the selection.

What You NEED

- ✓ Your book
- ✓ Sticky notes
- ✓ "Say Something" Organizer (choose one)
- ✓ "Say Something" Record Sheet (choose one)
- ✓ Pencil or pen

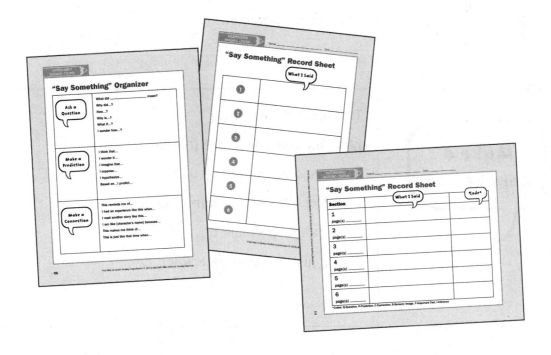

"Say Something" Organizer

Ask a Question	What did _____ mean? Why did…? How…? Why is…? What if…? I wonder how…?
Make a Prediction	I think that… I wonder if… I imagine that… I suppose… I hypothesize… Based on… I predict…
Make a Connection	This reminds me of… I had an experience like this when… I read another story like this… I am like [character's name] because… This makes me think of… This is just like that time when…

Fresh Takes on Centers: Reading Comprehension © 2010 by Mary Beth Allen. Scholastic Teaching Resources

"Say Something" Organizer

Explain a Sensory Image	In my mind I see… It makes me feel… I can smell… A picture that is emerging is… When it said… it made me think about… I can hear…
Tell an Important Fact	The important ideas so far… A new fact I have learned… I never knew… I want to remember… Something worth remembering is…
Make an Inference	Based on… I can infer… When the text says… it helps me know… When it said… I knew… because… The pictures help me know… because…

Name _____ Date _____

"Say Something" Record Sheet

What I Said

1	
2	
3	
4	
5	
6	

"Say Something" Record Sheet

Section	What I Said	Code*
1 page(s) _____		
2 page(s) _____		
3 page(s) _____		
4 page(s) _____		
5 page(s) _____		
6 page(s) _____		

*Codes: Q-Question, P-Prediction, C-Connection, S-Sensory Image, F-Important Fact, I-Inference

Visual Summaries

Description: This activity provides students with a visual strategy for recording information from a text. Students use sketches and labels as a way of recording story elements or important information gathered from reading.

Materials

✤ Student texts (fiction and informational)

✤ Student directions (page 114)

✤ Visual Summaries organizers (pages 115–117)

✤ Sticky notes

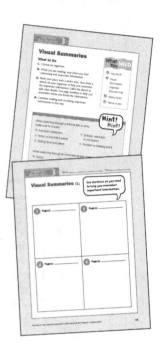

Procedures for Teaching

1. Choose a text to read aloud. Use a think-aloud approach to show how you identify and think about important information.

Teaching
↘ TIP

If you are using a fiction text, include representations of the following components:

- ◉ Important characters

- ◉ Setting (time and place)

- ◉ Problem or initiating event

- ◉ Action or important events

- ◉ Solution, resolution, or conclusion

If you are using an informational text, include representations of the following:

- ◉ Topics

- ◉ Main ideas

- ◉ Important facts and details from the text

2. Display the four-square Visual Summaries organizer (page 115) and give students a copy to follow along. Discuss and model ways to represent important information on the organizer using drawings and labels.

3. Read another section of text and guide students in identifying the important information. Discuss ways to represent this information using drawings and labels. Allow students time to sketch and label the information on their organizers. Remind them to record the page number.

4. Continue reading the text in sections. After each section, have students sketch the important information and record the page number. Encourage students to share ideas in pairs and with the class. Continue this process, gradually reducing the amount of support once students show they understand.

5. After reading, have students summarize the important content on their organizers in pairs or small groups. Then bring students together to summarize key information. Engage students in demonstrations or conversations about different ways they can represent information.

6. At another time, repeat the procedure to model using different types of text (fiction or informational) and to model using the other organizers (pages 116–117). Point out that the organizers with six and eight boxes are appropriate for recording more details and for longer texts.

7. For independent practice at the center, have students use the process of sketching through the text to document important information as they read.

Suggestions for Differentiated Learning

Provide More Support

- To guide students in identifying important information, use sticky notes to label text sections with questions or prompts or to identify key information.

- Enlarge the organizers to allow for larger sketches or more information.

- Help students label their sketches to support them in remembering important information.

Provide More Challenge

- Allow students to determine how many sketches they need to include to document all the important information.

- Have students write a caption or summary sentence for each sketch.

- Use the sketches as a plan to write summaries or create poems.

Visual Summaries

What to Do

1. Choose an organizer.

2. While you are reading, stop when you find interesting and important information.

3. Mark your place with a sticky note, then draw a sketch on your organizer to help you remember the important information. Label the sketch to add other details. List page numbers to help you remember where you found the information.

4. Continue reading and recording important information in this way.

What You NEED

- ✓ Your book
- ✓ Visual Summaries organizer (choose one)
- ✓ Sticky notes
- ✓ Pencil or pen

Hint! Hint!

When sketching through a fictional text or story, make sure to include:

⇨ Important characters

⇨ Action or important events

⇨ Setting (time and place)

⇨ Solution, resolution, or conclusion

⇨ Problem or initiating event

When sketching through an informational text, make sure to include:

⇨ Topics

⇨ Main ideas

⇨ Important facts and details

Name _____ Date _____

Visual Summaries (1)

Use sketches as you read to help you remember important information.

1 Page(s): _____	**2** Page(s): _____
3 Page(s): _____	**4** Page(s): _____

Name _____ Date _____

Visual Summaries (2)

Use sketches as you read to help you remember important information.

1 Page(s): _____	**2** Page(s): _____
3 Page(s): _____	**4** Page(s): _____
5 Page(s): _____	**6** Page(s): _____

Fresh Takes on Centers: Reading Comprehension © 2010 by Mary Beth Allen. Scholastic Teaching Resources

Name _____ Date _____

Visual Summaries (3)

Use sketches as you read to help you remember important information.

1 Page(s): _____	**2** Page(s): _____
3 Page(s): _____	**4** Page(s): _____
5 Page(s): _____	**6** Page(s): _____
7 Page(s): _____	**8** Page(s): _____

Summary Boxes

Description: Students use graphic organizers to document the key elements of a story or the most important facts from an informational text.

Materials

❖ Student texts

❖ Student directions (page 120)

❖ Summary Boxes organizers (pages 121–122)

Procedures for Teaching

1. Display and review each Summary Boxes organizer (Narrative Summary Boxes and Informational Summary Boxes).

2. Model completing a Summary Boxes organizer with a read-aloud to show how to represent important information using pictures and sentences. Begin with the first box and use a think-aloud to model how to capture—in pictures, labels, and sentences—the information needed in that box.

3. Continue to read, involving students in assisting you with completing the remainder of the chart. Prompt as needed.

4. Allow students to practice completing a chart independently or with a partner after listening to another text.

5. Repeat the process to model using both the Narrative and Informational Summary Boxes organizers.

6. For independent practice at the center, encourage students to use the Summary Boxes organizers after reading as a way to document their understanding of the text.

Additional Ideas for Using the Summary Boxes Organizers

Modify the prompt questions in each of the boxes to help students identify key information from an expository text. Sample questions for two new organizers follow.

Informational Summary Boxes: Geography (State)

✤ Where?

✤ What are the symbols?

✤ What are some major cities?

✤ What makes it special?

Informational Summary Boxes: Living Things

✤ What does it look like?

✤ Where does it live?

✤ What does it need for survival?

✤ What's an interesting fact?

Suggestions for Differentiated Learning

Provide More Support

◉ Provide clues, words, or questions to guide thinking and focus students on the important information.

◉ Choose texts that have obvious text elements or that have subtitles to guide thinking.

◉ Color-code each section (for example, with different-colored sticky notes) to guide students to look at one section at a time.

Provide More Challenge

◉ Include more sections on the organizers to encourage students to record more details. Have students also identify the main idea or theme.

◉ Have students use the information in the boxes as an organizer for writing a summary.

◉ Allow students to create their own boxes to capture the main idea.

Summary Boxes

What to Do

1. Choose a Summary Boxes organizer to match what you are reading.

2. After reading your text, use the organizer to summarize the most important information. Use drawing and words to complete each box.

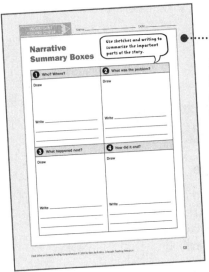

Use the Narrative Summary Boxes organizer if you are reading a story.

What You NEED

- ✓ Your book
- ✓ Summary Boxes organizer (choose one)
- ✓ Pencil or pen

Use the Informational Summary Boxes organizer if you are reading a piece of nonfiction.

Hint! Hint!

Add labels to your drawings as a way to include more information or other important details.

Fresh Takes on Centers: Reading Comprehension © 2010 by Mary Beth Allen. Scholastic Teaching Resources

Name _____ Date _____

Narrative Summary Boxes

Use sketches and writing to summarize the important parts of the story.

1 Who? Where?	**2** What was the problem?
Draw Write _____ _____ _____	Draw Write _____ _____ _____
3 What happened next?	**4** How did it end?
Draw Write _____ _____ _____	Draw Write _____ _____ _____

Name _____ Date _____

Informational Summary Boxes

Use sketches and writing to summarize the important parts of the story.

1 Important Fact	**2** Important Fact
Draw	**Draw**
Write _____	**Write** _____
_____	_____
_____	_____

3 Important Fact	**4** Important Fact
Draw	**Draw**
Write _____	**Write** _____
_____	_____
_____	_____

Fresh Takes on Centers: Reading Comprehension © 2010 by Mary Beth Allen. Scholastic Teaching Resources

Summary Pyramids

Description: Students use a structured format to summarize the key content of a story or informational text.

Materials

✤ Student texts

✤ Chart paper

✤ Student directions (page 125)

✤ Summary Pyramid organizers (pages 126–127)

✤ Thesaurus (optional)

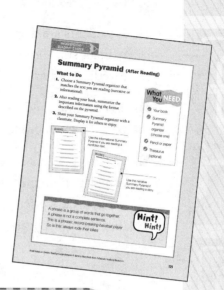

Procedures for Teaching

1. On chart paper, show students the format for writing informational and narrative pyramids.

Informational Pyramid

Line 1: topic

Line 2: two adjectives describing the topic

Line 3: three-word phrase describing action of the topic

Line 4: four-word phrase stating an important fact about the topic

Line 5: five-word phrase stating an important fact about the topic

Line 6: six-word phrase stating another important fact about the topic

Line 7: seven-word phrase stating a fourth important fact about the topic

Line 8: eight-word phrase telling something else you would like to learn or
   a question you have about the topic

Narrative Pyramid

Line 1: character's name

Line 2: two words describing the character

Line 3: three-word phrase describing the setting

Line 4: four-word phrase stating the problem or goal

Line 5: five-word phrase describing one important event

Line 6: six-word phrase describing another important event

Line 7: seven-word phrase describing a third important event

Line 8: eight-word phrase describing the solution or how the story ended

---

2. After reading a text aloud, model the process of creating a Summary Pyramid by thinking aloud about the important information suggested for each line. Complete the first few lines as a demonstration. Model using a thesaurus to find interesting words you can use.

3. Use guiding questions to help students complete the next several lines as a class. Reduce the amount of guiding as students show they understand the process.

4. If students are demonstrating that they understand, allow them to work in pairs or small groups to complete the last line or two. Then, bring students together to share ideas with the class.

5. To encourage independence, have students create summary pyramids in pairs or small groups after reading a common text.

6. For independent practice, place Summary Pyramid organizers and completed samples at the center. Have students create pyramids to summarize stories or texts they have read. Provide space for students to display their pyramids if they wish.

Suggestions for Differentiated Learning

Provide More Support

- Modify the pyramid to require fewer responses.

- Have students work with a partner.

- Provide a word or two to start each line of the pyramid.

Provide More Challenge

- Have students create pyramids from different points of view.

- Have students use a thesaurus or other reference tools to strengthen word choice.

- Allow students to create their own topics for each line of the pyramid.

Summary Pyramid (After Reading)

What to Do

1. Choose a Summary Pyramid organizer that matches the text you are reading (informational or narrative).

2. After reading your book, summarize the important information using the format described on the pyramid.

3. Share your Summary Pyramid organizer with a classmate. Display it for others to enjoy.

What You NEED

- ✓ Your book
- ✓ Summary Pyramid organizers (choose one)
- ✓ Pencil or paper
- ✓ Thesaurus (optional)

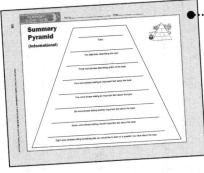

Use the informational Summary Pyramid if you are reading a nonfiction text.

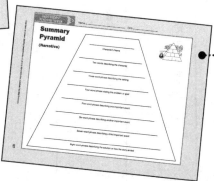

Use the narrative Summary Pyramid if you are reading a story.

A phrase is a group of words that go together.
A phrase is not a complete sentence.
This is a phrase: *record-breaking baseball player*
So is this: *always rode their bikes*

Hint! Hint!

Summary
Pyramid
(Informational)

Name _____   Date _____

Topic _____

Two adjectives describing the topic

Three-word phrase describing action of the topic

Four-word phrase stating an important fact about the topic

Five-word phrase stating an important fact about the topic

Six-word phrase stating another important fact about the topic

Seven-word phrase stating a fourth important fact about the topic

Eight word phrases telling something else you would like to learn or a question you have about the topic

Summary
Pyramid
(Narrative)

Character's Name

Two words describing the character

Three-word phrase describing the setting

Four-word phrase stating the problem or goal

Five-word phrase describing one important event

Six-word phrase describing another important event

Seven-word phrase describing a third important event

Eight-word phrase describing the solution or how the story ended

Thinking Through the Text

Description: Students read sections of text and document thinking while they are reading, focusing on important information, questions, predictions, and inferences.

Materials

✤ Student texts

✤ Student directions (page 130)

✤ Thinking Through the Text organizers (pages 131–133)

Procedures for Teaching

1. Explain to students that it is essential that they actively think while reading. Discuss strategies related to using information in the text to guide thinking about what will come or happen later in the text. For example, students may be aware that headings in nonfiction texts help them predict what the main idea of that section will be.

2. Choose a book and a Thinking Through the Text organizer. Review the organizer, then model the process of thinking about the text, starting with the cover, if possible. Complete the organizer to document your thinking about important information, questions, predictions, and inferences.

3. Read a section of text aloud. Think aloud about the new information that has been discovered and questions that have been answered. Again, record important information, and use that information to think about new questions, predictions, and inferences.

4. When students understand the process, prompt as needed to have them identify important information in the next section of text. Add their ideas to the organizer and guide them to use that information to create new questions, predictions, and inferences.

5. As students gain competency, gradually reduce the amount of guidance. Allow students to work in pairs or groups with a text and an organizer, and to share their ideas for thinking through a text.

6. Review how to use other versions of the Thinking Through the Text organizers. For independent practice at the center, have students use the organizers to document their thinking during reading.

Suggestions for Differentiated Learning

Provide More Support

⊙ Provide clues as to the important information.

⊙ Read the text in small segments.

⊙ Use prompts to guide thinking— for example, "I learned _____. This makes me predict _____."

Provide More Challenge

⊙ Use more complex texts.

⊙ Have students document the thinking after each chapter of a novel.

⊙ Introduce additional ways of thinking about the text—for example, visualizing and clarifying ideas and words.

Thinking Through the Text

What to Do

1. Choose an organizer. Before reading, look at the cover illustration and title of the book and record what you know. Use that information to list questions, predictions, or inferences about the text.

2. Read a section of text, and record important information you have learned. Use that information to think about and record new questions, predictions, and inferences you are thinking about the text.

3. Continue reading and thinking through the text to complete the organizer.

What You NEED

- ✓ Your book
- ✓ Thinking Through the Text organizers (choose one)
- ✓ Pencil or pen

Hint! Hint!

People make inferences every day. If you see someone put on a bike helmet, you can *infer* that person is going for a bike ride. If your teacher tells everyone to line up at the door, you can infer the class is going somewhere.

When you make inferences about a text, you are "reading between the lines." The author doesn't come right out and state something. But you can use the information that's there to figure out something. Making inferences when you read helps you better understand the text.

    Fresh Takes on Centers: Reading Comprehension © 2010 by Mary Beth Allen. Scholastic Teaching Resources

Name _____ Date _____

Thinking Through the Text

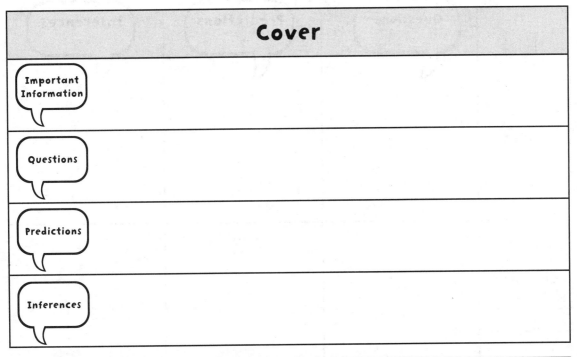

Cover

Important Information	
Questions	
Predictions	
Inferences	

Chapter/Pages: _____

Important Information	
Questions	
Predictions	
Inferences	

Name _____ Date _____

Thinking Through the Text

	Questions ...	Predictions ...	Inferences ...
Cover			
Chapter/ Pages: _____			
Chapter/ Pages: _____			
Chapter/ Pages: _____			

Fresh Takes on Centers: Reading Comprehension © 2010 by Mary Beth Allen. Scholastic Teaching Resources

Thinking Through the Text

Before Reading

I predict _____
_____
because _____
_____.

During Reading

Read to page _____
I now predict _____
_____
because _____
_____.

During Reading

Read to page _____
I now predict _____
_____
because _____
_____.

During Reading

Read to page _____
I now predict _____
_____
because _____
_____.

After Reading

I feel _____
_____
because _____
_____.

Setting Up a Vocabulary Center

A center that focuses on words makes vocabulary practice playful and fun. The Vocabulary Center activities in this section provide opportunities for students to explore words using graphic organizers, games, and other resources. In the process, students will build connections between and among words, try out new words, and enrich and expand their vocabulary.

Connections to the Standards

The center activities in this section support the following standards for students in grades 3–5, outlined by Mid-continent Research for Education and Learning (McREL), an organization that collects and synthesizes national and state K–12 curriculum standards.

Reading
Uses the general skills and strategies of the reading process

- Uses phonetic and structural analysis techniques, syntactic structure, and semantic context to decode unknown words
- Use a variety of context clues to decode unknown words
- Uses word reference materials, such as a dictionary or thesaurus, to understand unknown words
- Understands level-appropriate reading vocabulary
- Monitors own reading strategies and makes modifications as needed
- Uses a variety of strategies to extend reading vocabulary (e.g., uses analogies, idioms, similes, metaphors to infer the meaning of literal and figurative phrases; uses definition, restatement, example, comparison and contrast to verify word meanings; identifies shades of meaning; knows denotative and connotative meanings; knows vocabulary related to different content areas and current events; uses rhyming dictionaries, classification books, etymological dictionaries)

Source: *Content Knowledge: A Compendium of Standards and Benchmarks for K–12 Education* (4th ed.). Mid-continent Research for Education and Learning, 2004 (http://www.mcrel.org/standards–benchmarks).

Teaching ↘ TIP

To keep this center fresh throughout the school year, modify activities and vocabulary topics and word lists to connect with content area and literature studies.

Vocabulary Center Materials

❖ Vocabulary Center Self-Assessment (page 137)

❖ Reproducible student pages

❖ Samples of completed activities

❖ Resources for working with words (dictionaries, picture dictionaries, rhyming dictionaries, thesauruses)

❖ Pictures and other visuals to spark thinking and discussion about language

❖ Student work samples

❖ Sticky notes

Teaching the Process

Students can learn to be intrigued by words if they have the opportunity to use them in a safe context. All activities at the center first need to be taught using a direct instruction process of modeling, guiding, and gradually releasing responsibility to the students. Use the following procedures to make sure all your students can work at the Vocabulary Center independently.

1. Choose a Vocabulary Center activity sheet. Show students how they should read through the student directions first to get ready to complete the activity. Preview the activity page and think aloud about how you will complete it.

2. Demonstrate how to complete the activity, thinking aloud about words as you do so. Show the thinking and decisions needed to complete the task.

3. Repeat steps 1–2 with other Vocabulary Center activities. As students demonstrate they understand the processes, guide them to participate in completing a new activity with you, thinking aloud about new words and the steps involved in using the record sheets and resources. Provide hints and prompts that will guarantee them success.

4. When you feel students understand the process, allow individuals or groups to work with selected activities. Observe students to determine if they need more or less support.

Teaching ↘ TIP

As you prepare to introduce a center activity, preview the lesson (Procedures for Teaching) to determine the amount of time you will need to spend on the material. Many activities are best taught over a period of several days.

5. If students seem to be able to engage successfully with the vocabulary activities, then it is appropriate for them to practice the activities at the Vocabulary Center. If students are unable to work with them successfully, provide further modeling until they can complete them on their own.

6. Display and review the Vocabulary Center Self-Assessment. Remind students that when completing the self-assessment form, there may be times when not all categories will apply. For example, if using pictures and context is enough to help with a new word, students may not end up also using a dictionary or thesaurus. In this case, they would leave number 4 blank, or write a note explaining that they did not require those resources to complete the activity.

Adapting the Process

With the appropriate support or challenge, all students can extend their reading, writing, and speaking vocabularies by working and playing with words in a successful way. Each center activity in this section includes suggestions for providing more support or an extra challenge. In addition, keep the following suggestions for differentiated learning in mind.

Suggestions for Differentiated Learning

Provide More Support

- Modify the organizers so fewer responses are required.
- Mark pages in the dictionary or thesaurus to guide students' explorations.
- Use picture dictionaries.
- Allow students to work with a more knowledgeable partner.

Provide More Challenge

- Encourage independent use of dictionaries and thesauruses to find interesting and vivid vocabulary.
- Have students work with more challenging or abstract words.
- Allow students to share new words with classmates.
- Have students extend work with roots, prefixes, and suffixes.

Vocabulary Center
Self-Assessment

	Basic	Good	Great
1. I followed the directions for each activity.			
2. I found new and interesting words. Examples:			
3. I used pictures and context to help figure out the meaning of new words.			
4. I used a dictionary or thesaurus to help understand new words.			
5. I documented my learning by writing and using new words.			

While working at this center I learned:

_____

_____

_____

Next time I would like to try: _____

_____

_____

Sketch a Word

Description: Students draw sketches to represent the meanings of words—such as multiple-meaning words, synonyms, antonyms, homonyms, words with common roots, story vocabulary, and words related to a content area.

Materials

✦ Chart paper

✦ Student directions (page 140)

✦ Sketch a Word graphic organizers (pages 141–144; enlarge to provide additional space for drawing and writing)

✦ Dictionary

Procedures for Teaching

1. Choose a word to sketch, such as a multiple-meaning word. Use the word in context—for example, "The children gathered around to hear their teacher read a new **story**" and "The new three-**story** building has shops and apartments."

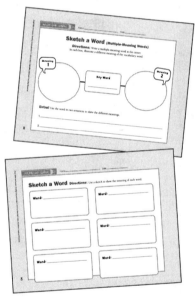

2. Invite students to explain what the word means in each sentence. Use a dictionary to confirm the meaning.

3. On chart paper (or another visual display), model the process of sketching each meaning of the word. Use the format of one of the multiple-meaning word organizers.

4. Have students work with a partner to sketch a new multiple-meaning word (using the same format modeled in step 3). Guide as needed. Encourage students to discuss different meanings of the word before sketching.

Teaching ↘ TIP

For a variation on this activity, students can sketch both the literal and figurative meaning of idiomatic expressions such as "a piece of cake," "on pins and needles," and "under the weather."

138

5. Repeat steps 1–4 to provide practice with other types of words (such as synonyms, antonyms, words with common roots, story vocabulary, and words from a content area study) and other organizer formats.

6. For independent practice at the center, post vocabulary words for students to sketch. These might include the following:

✤ words from a unit of study

✤ multiple-meaning words

✤ synonyms or antonyms

✤ roots

✤ words borrowed from other countries (such as *adobe*, *bangle*, *bizarre*).

Suggestions for Differentiated Learning

Provide More Support

◉ Use words that are more familiar or concrete.

◉ Use words in sentences to provide meaning clues.

◉ Guide students to determine the most effective organizer for their word.

Provide More Challenge

◉ Have students find examples of types of words you are using. For example, if you model the activity using a multiple-meaning word, have them generate a list of other multiple-meaning words and create sketches for them.

◉ Have students write a sentence to go with their sketch (or two sentences if multiple meanings are involved).

◉ Have students share sketches with classmates to see who can guess the word.

Sketch a Word

What to Do

1. Read the vocabulary words on the list. Choose a word or words to sketch.

2. Use a dictionary to check your understanding of the words.

3. Think of a way to represent the meaning of the words in a sketch.

4. Choose a Sketch a Word organizer (or use the one assigned). Complete it as directed to show the meaning of the words. Use labels to provide additional information about word meaning.

5. Optional: Write a sentence to go with your sketch or sketches.

What You NEED

- ✓ Sketch a Word graphic organizers (choose one)
- ✓ Pencil or pen
- ✓ Dictionary

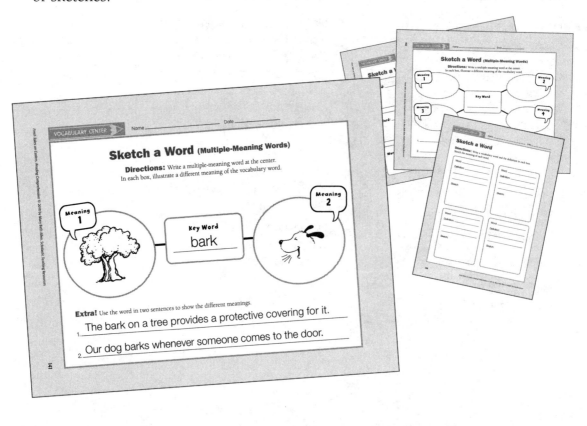

Fresh Takes on Centers: Reading Comprehension © 2010 by Mary Beth Allen. Scholastic Teaching Resources

▷ VOCABULARY CENTER

Sketch a Word (Multiple-Meaning Words)

Directions: Write a multiple-meaning word at the center.
In each box, illustrate a different meaning of the vocabulary word.

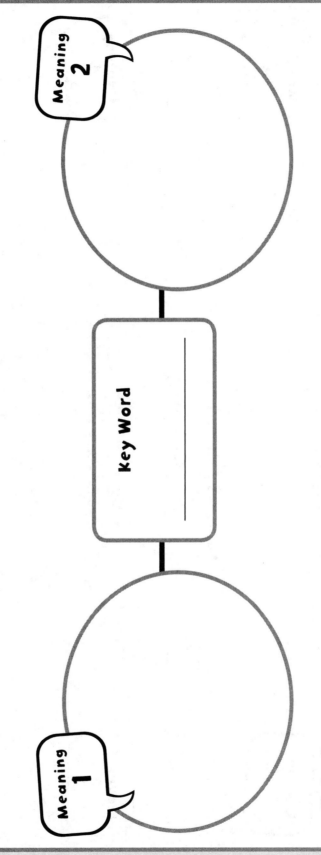

Meaning 2

Key Word
_____

Meaning 1

Extra! Use the word in two sentences to show the different meanings.

1. _____

2. _____

Sketch a Word (Multiple-Meaning Words)

Directions: Write a multiple-meaning word at the center.
In each box, illustrate a different meaning of the vocabulary word.

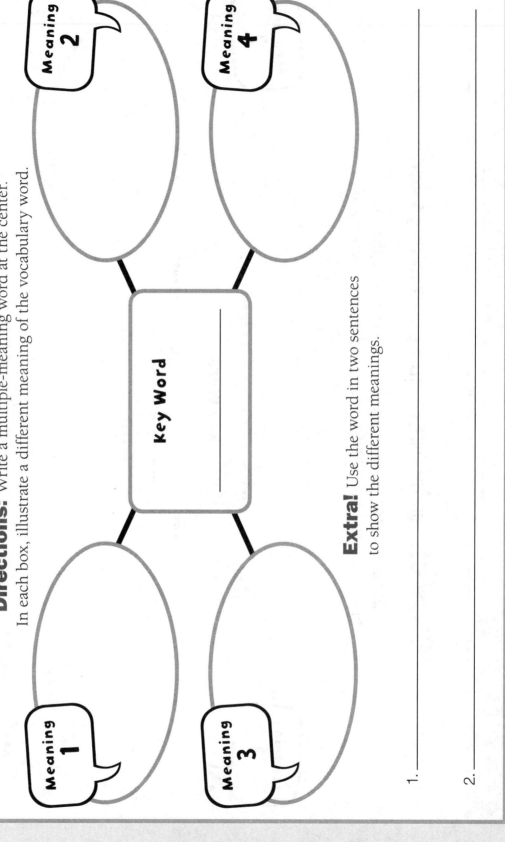

Meaning 2

Meaning 4

Meaning 1

Meaning 3

Key Word

Extra! Use the word in two sentences
to show the different meanings.

1. _____

2. _____

Fresh Takes on Centers: Reading Comprehension © 2010 by Mary Beth Allen. Scholastic Teaching Resources

Sketch a Word

Directions: Use a sketch to show the meaning of each word.

Word: _____

Word: _____

Word: _____

Word: _____

Word: _____

Word: _____

Name _____ Date _____

Sketch a Word

Directions: Write a vocabulary word and the definition in each box. Sketch the meaning of each word.

Word: _____

Definition: _____

_____

_____

Sketch:

Word: _____

Definition: _____

_____

_____

Sketch:

Word: _____

Definition: _____

_____

_____

Sketch:

Word: _____

Definition: _____

_____

_____

Sketch:

 Fresh Takes on Centers: Reading Comprehension © 2010 by Mary Beth Allen. Scholastic Teaching Resources

Word Maps

Description: Students connect words and ideas to a key word as a way to build a personal understanding.

Materials

✦ Student directions (page 147)

✦ Word Maps (pages 148–153)

✦ Dictionary and thesaurus

Procedures for Teaching

1. Choose a key word (or root or affix) that is new and interesting for students. This can come from a content area or from a text they are reading. Introduce the word (or root or affix) in the context of a sentence or paragraph.

2. Think aloud about what you know about the word and what the context tells you. Model using a dictionary (or other reference tool) to learn more about the word.

3. Then choose and introduce one of the Word Maps (Word Connections, Word Associations, Synonyms, Antonyms, Multiple Connections, Word Investigation) and explain the setup.

4. Using the ideas you have thought about, model how to complete the Word Map. Guide students to help you.

5. Introduce a new word. Have students work in groups to complete the same Word Map used in step 3, then share their ideas with the class.

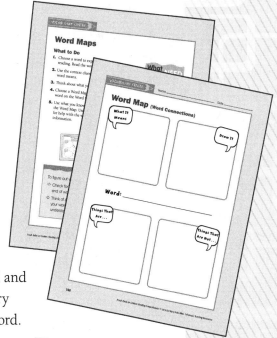

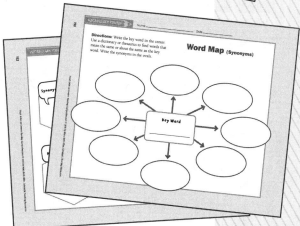

6. Over a period of several days, repeat steps 1–5 to introduce other Word Maps.

7. For independent practice at the Vocabulary Center, allow individuals to complete Word Maps and share their ideas with partners or small groups.

Suggestions for Differentiated Learning

Provide More Support

- Provide definitions and pictures. Use words in sentences.

- Provide additional information about each word. For example, make connections to what students already know.

- Model with one word and have students complete the task independently with a similar word or synonym.

Provide More Challenge

- Encourage students to use interesting, unusual, or abstract vocabulary in each section.

- Provide reference tools to support use of interesting and challenging words.

- Have students extend work by using words with specific roots, prefixes, or suffixes.

Word Maps

What to Do

1. Choose a word to explore from a text you are reading. Read the word in the sentence.

2. Use the context clues to figure out what the key word means.

3. Think about what you know about the key word.

4. Choose a Word Map to complete. Write the key word on the Word Map.

5. Use what you know about the word to complete the Word Map. Use a dictionary and thesaurus for help with the word meaning and other information.

What You NEED

- ✓ A text you are reading
- ✓ Word Maps (choose one)
- ✓ Pencil or pen
- ✓ Dictionary and thesaurus

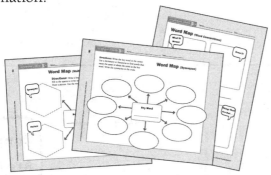

Hint! Hint!

To figure out what a word means, try these ideas:

⇒ Check for prefixes and suffixes at the beginning and end of words. This can help you identify the root.

⇒ Think of a word you know that is like a new word. For example, if your word is *geologist*, you might think of *geology*. This can help you understand that a geologist is someone who studies the earth.

Name _____ Date _____

Word Map (Word Connections)

What It Means

Draw It

Word: _____

Things That Are . . .

Things That Are Not . . .

Name _____ Date _____

Word Map (Word Associations)

Word

Draw It

Definition

Associations

Word Map (Synonyms)

Directions: Write the key word in the center. Use a dictionary or thesaurus to find words that mean the same or about the same as the key word. Write the synonyms in the ovals.

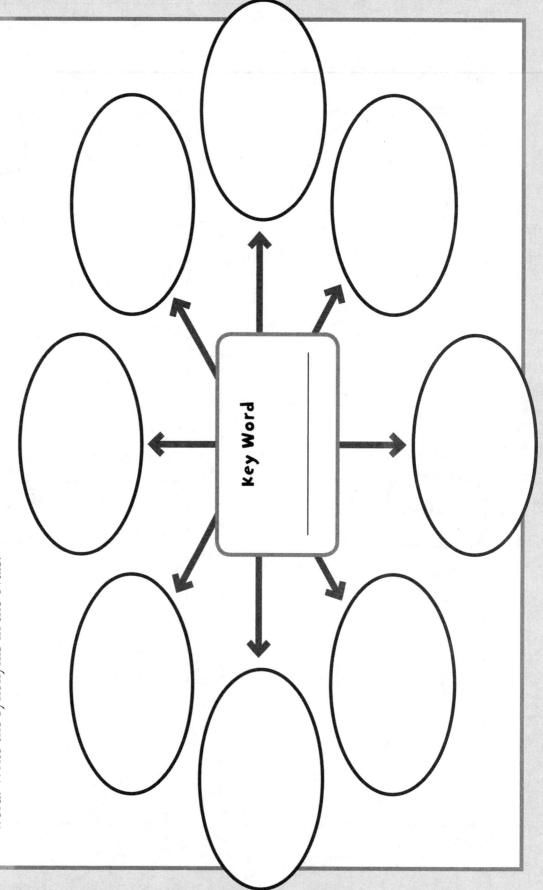

Key Word

Word Map (Antonyms)

Directions: Write a key word at the center. Use a dictionary or thesaurus to find words that mean the opposite of the key word. Write the antonyms in the ovals.

Key Word _____

VOCABULARY CENTER

Word Map (Multiple Connections)

Directions: Write a key word at the center.
Fill in the spaces to write synonyms and antonyms.
Draw a picture. Use the word in a sentence.

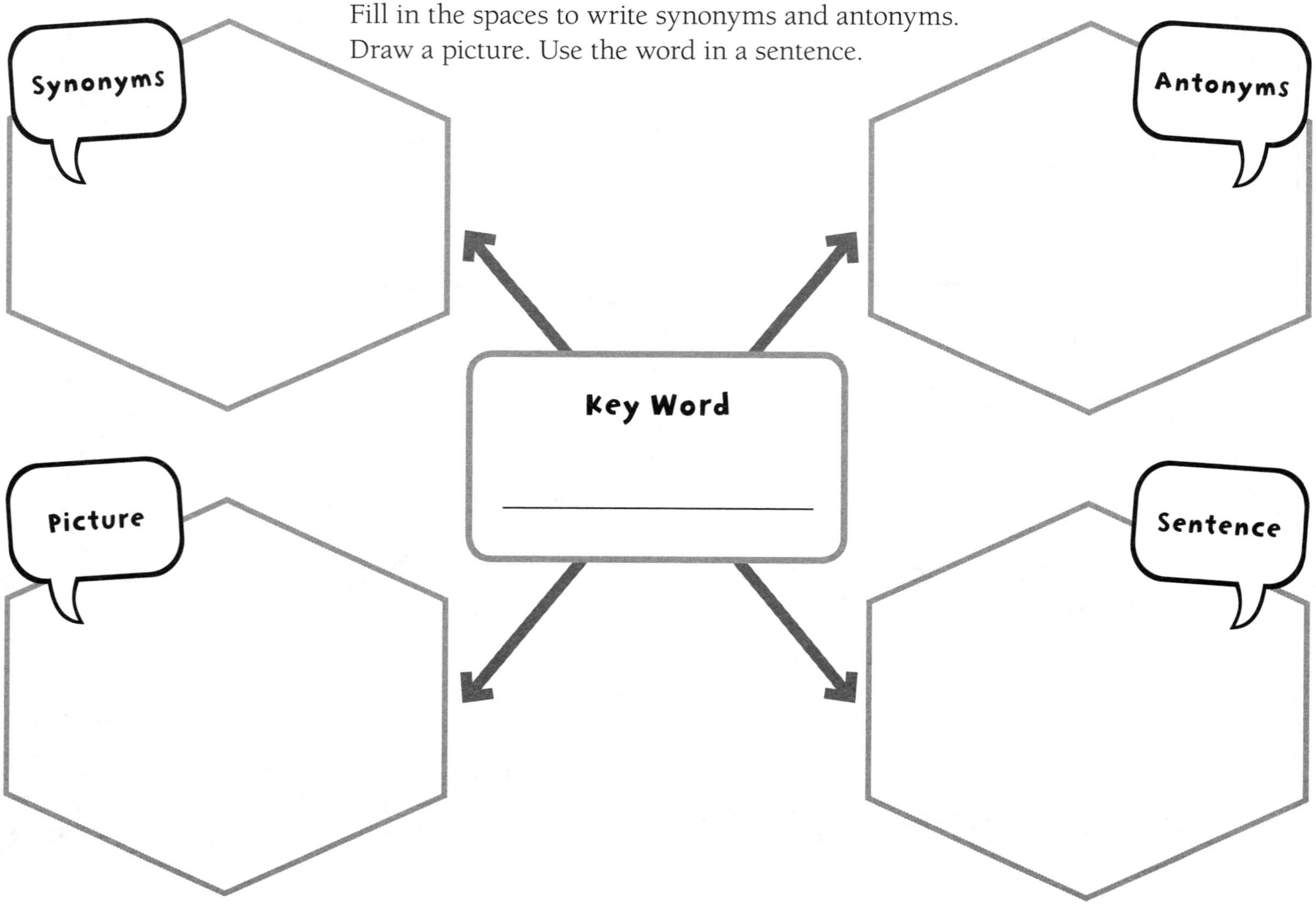

Antonyms

Sentence

Key Word
_____

Synonyms

Picture

Fresh Takes on Centers: Reading Comprehension © 2010 by Mary Beth Allen. Scholastic Teaching Resources

VOCABULARY CENTER

Word Map: Word Investigation

Word Parts

Root:

Prefix:

Suffix:

**Related Words
(Synonyms)**

Key Word: _____

Definition: _____
_____
_____

**Etymology
(Word Origin)**

Picture and Sentence

Alphabet Organizer

Description: Students identify words related to a topic, finding one or more words for each letter of the alphabet.

Materials

✤ Student texts (informational)

✤ Student directions (page 155)

✤ Alphabet Organizer (page 156)

Procedures for Teaching

1. Choose a familiar informational text and think aloud about the topic. Model the process of using the Alphabet Organizer to record words you know that are related to that topic.

2. As you read aloud the text, pause to add new words to the organizer. Encourage students to contribute words as well.

3. Continue reading, eventually having students work in pairs or small groups to come up with words on their own.

4. For independent practice, place copies of the Alphabet Organizer at the center. Post a topic and stock the center with related books and other resources. Have students use the resources to complete an Alphabet Organizer.

Suggestions for Differentiated Learning

Provide More Support

◉ Provide pictures or a picture walk to help students generate language related to the topic.

◉ Provide students with words related to the topic and allow them to sort the words alphabetically on the organizer.

Provide More Challenge

◉ Encourage students to use inferences to identify related words (words not in the text).

◉ Have students identify two or more words for each letter. Enlarge the organizer to provide more space for writing.

Teaching TIP

As you model completing an Alphabet Organizer, take time to discuss the meaning of words you add. This will benefit students who may be unfamiliar with the words and provide review for others.

Alphabet Organizer

What to Do

1. Think about the assigned topic. What words come to mind?

2. Use the first letter of each word you think of to determine what box to write the word in. For example, if you are thinking about weather you could write the word **evaporation** in the **E** box.

3. Continue brainstorming words related to the topic. Try to fill in as many boxes as possible.

4. Now, read about the topic. Add new words that you learn from the text to your Alphabet Organizer.

5. Try to think of at least one word for every letter box.

What You NEED

- ✓ Reading material on the topic
- ✓ Alphabet Organizer
- ✓ Pencil or pen

Hint! Hint!

Be creative when you're trying to fill in boxes for each letter. For example, if your topic is "water," you might write "nearly colorless" for the letter **N**.

Name _____ Date _____

Alphabet Organizer

Topic: _____

A	B
C	D	E
F	G	H
I	J	K
L	M	N
O	P	Q
R	S	T
U	V	W
X	Y	Z

Fresh Takes on Centers: Reading Comprehension © 2010 by Mary Beth Allen. Scholastic Teaching Resources

Vocabulary Brainstorm

Description: Students use a visual cue to brainstorm a variety of kinds of words (nouns, verbs, adjectives, adverbs, etc.). They then use some of those words to write a descriptive sentence or paragraph about the picture.

Materials

✤ Pictures related to topics of study

✤ Student directions (page 159)

✤ Vocabulary Brainstorm organizer (page 160)

✤ Dictionary and thesaurus

Procedures for Teaching

1. Review parts of speech with students, including nouns, verbs, and adjectives (and others such as adverbs and prepositions).

2. Display a picture or other visual cue. (Postcards, calendars, wordless picture books, and the Internet are good resources for interesting pictures.) Think aloud to model how to use the picture to generate words that describe it. Record words in the appropriate box on the Vocabulary Brainstorm organizer.

3. Invite students to add words for each category. Encourage them to use a dictionary or thesaurus, if needed.

4. Once there are several words in each box, model how to use some of those words to create a sentence about the picture. Allow students to add ideas or help with editing.

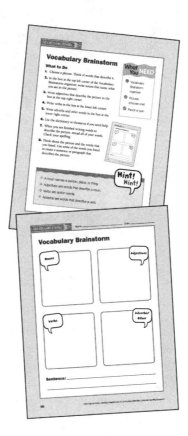

5. Have students work in pairs or small groups to use the words from the organizer in new sentences. Invite students to share their sentences with the class.

6. For independent practice at the center, select and display pictures and other visual cues, and have students complete Vocabulary Brainstorm organizers to explore related vocabulary. To complete the activity, have students use some of their words in sentences (or paragraphs).

Suggestions for Differentiated Learning

Provide More Support

- Have students first write words on sticky notes or index cards and then arrange them to help form sentences.

- Have students dictate sentences for scribing.

- Provide students with a word or two in each section to get them started.

Provide More Challenge

- Encourage students to use their words to write short paragraphs about the pictures.

- Have students use dictionaries and thesauruses to make their word lists more vivid.

- Have students use as many of the words as they can to make an effective sentence.

Vocabulary Brainstorm

What to Do

1. Choose a picture. Think of words that describe it.

2. In the box at the top left corner of the Vocabulary Brainstorm organizer, write nouns that name what you see in the picture.

3. Write adjectives that describe the picture in the box at the top right corner.

4. Write verbs in the box at the lower left corner.

5. Write adverbs and other words in the box at the lower right corner.

6. Use the dictionary or thesaurus if you need help.

7. When you are finished writing words to describe the picture, reread all of your words. Check your spelling.

8. Think about the picture and the words that you listed. Use some of the words you listed to create a sentence or paragraph that describes the picture.

What You NEED

- ✔ Vocabulary Brainstorm organizer
- ✔ Pictures (choose one)
- ✔ Pencil or pen

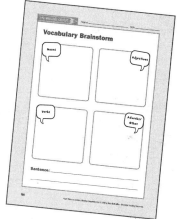

⇒ A noun names a person, place, or thing.

⇒ Adjectives are words that describe a noun.

⇒ Verbs are action words.

⇒ Adverbs are words that describe a verb.

Name _____ Date _____

Vocabulary Brainstorm

Sentence: _____

_____

Fresh Takes on Centers: Reading Comprehension © 2010 by Mary Beth Allen. Scholastic Teaching Resources

Word Sort

Description: Students group vocabulary words according to common characteristics.

Materials

- ✤ Student texts

- ✤ Student directions (page 163)

- ✤ Word Sort Cards (page 164)

- ✤ Word Sort Record Sheet (page 165)

Procedures for Teaching

1. In advance, select vocabulary words from a text or topic to be studied. These can represent a mix of challenging and more familiar words. Write each word on a word card. Write the topic at the top of the Word Sort Cards sheet.

2. Introduce the vocabulary words. Invite students to tell what they know about each word. Provide clarification about any of the words, as needed.

3. Cut apart the cards and model grouping several words by a common characteristic. For example, the words *waddle*, *slide*, and *swim* all describe the way penguins move.

4. Demonstrate placing the cards for those words in a pile and using the Word Sort Record Sheet to record how they sorted the words.

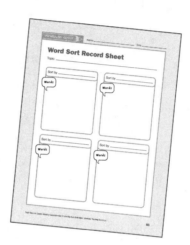

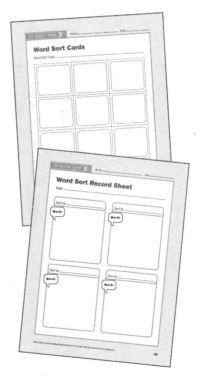

Teaching ↘ TIP

Figuring out how to group vocabulary words according to common characteristics helps students make meaningful connections among words, helps them build word knowledge, and helps them anticipate categories of information they will learn.

5. Identify several other words from the original set and have students work with a partner or in small groups to decide what common characteristic they share. Provide hints or prompts, as needed.

6. Have students work with partners or in small groups to sort remaining words, then share ideas with the class.

7. For independent practice at the center, provide sets of assorted Word Sort Cards (representing different topics) for students to cut apart and sort.

Suggestions for Differentiated Learning

Provide More Support

- Use a "closed sort" setup: Provide the categories and have students sort the words accordingly.

- Reduce the number of words for students to sort.

Provide More Challenge

- Use more sophisticated words.

- Encourage students to sort the words in multiple ways, for example, by topic or category, type (noun, verb, adjective, etc.), root, or affix.

Word Sort

What to Do

1. Choose a Word Sort Cards sheet. Read all of the words. Then cut apart the cards.

2. Think about what you know about each word and what some of the words have in common.

3. Sort the word cards into groups.

4. Write the words in each group on a Word Sort Record Sheet. Label each group according to what the words have in common.

5. Once you have sorted the words, try to think of another way you could sort them. Make new piles and complete a new record sheet.

What You NEED

- ✓ Word Sort Cards
- ✓ Scissors
- ✓ Word Sort Record Sheet
- ✓ Pencil or pen

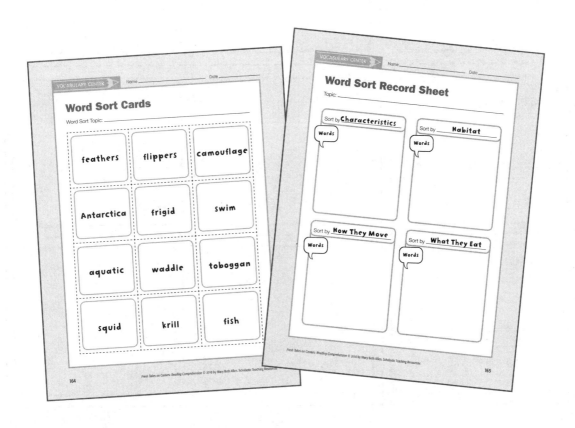

Name _____ Date _____

Word Sort Cards

Word Sort Topic: _____

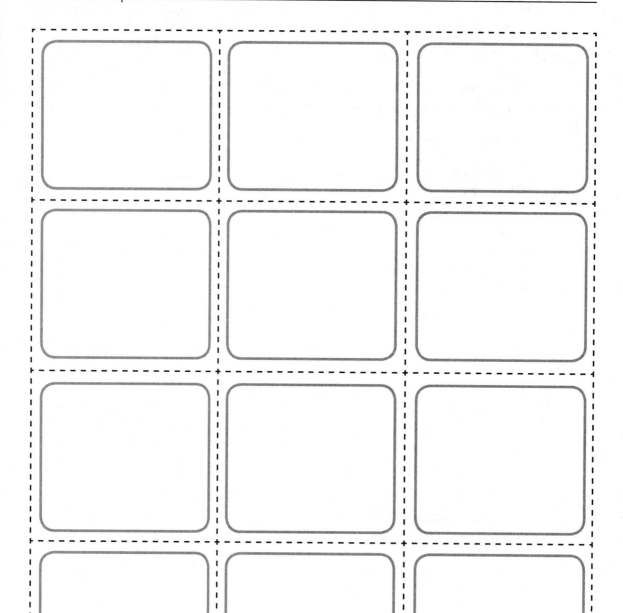

Fresh Takes on Centers: Reading Comprehension © 2010 by Mary Beth Allen. Scholastic Teaching Resources

Name _____ Date _____

Word Sort Record Sheet

Topic: _____

Sort by _____

Sort by _____

Words

Sort by _____

Sort by _____

Words

Vocabulary Memory Game

Description: Students match vocabulary words with pictures or meanings.

Materials

✤ Student directions (page 168)

✤ Vocabulary Memory Game Cards (page 169)

✤ Vocabulary Memory Game Record Sheet (page 170)

Procedures for Teaching

1. In advance, prepare a set of game cards as follows.

✤ Use the Vocabulary Memory Game Cards template to create a set of vocabulary cards. These words can come from content areas, a text students are reading, or from other areas of the curriculum or student interests.

✤ Write vocabulary words on one set of cards and put matching definitions (or synonyms or antonyms), fill-in-the blanks (cloze sentences), or pictures on a second set.

✤ Laminate cards for durability.

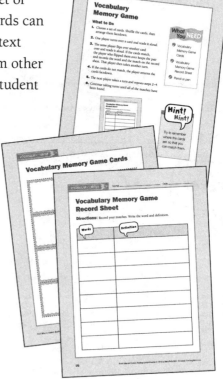

2. Review the words with students, then shuffle all cards and arrange them facedown in an array.

3. Model the process of playing the Vocabulary Memory Game. Turn over one card, read it, and then turn over another card. If the cards match, you get to keep the pair. If they do not match, place them facedown again.

4. Continue to turn over cards, two at a time, trying to find a match. Model your thinking about how to decide if the cards are a match. Also model how to remember where the match might be.

5. Invite students to take turns playing the game with you.

6. For independent practice, place sets of word cards at the center for students to use with partners or in small groups. To document their thinking, have students record words and matches on the record sheet.

Suggestions for Differentiated Learning

Provide More Support

⦿ Use fewer words.

⦿ Color-code each set of cards (so students can select one card of each color to try to make a match).

⦿ Have students match words and pictures, and then use their words in a sentence.

Provide More Challenge

⦿ Use synonyms, antonyms, category words, or other extensions of the words.

⦿ Allow students to make sets of cards for classmates to use at the center.

⦿ Use content-related words and have students match words with definitions or pictures.

Vocabulary Memory Game

What to Do

1. Choose a set of cards. Shuffle the cards, then arrange them facedown.

2. One player turns over a card and reads it aloud.

3. The same player flips over another card over and reads it aloud. If the cards match, the player who flipped them over keeps the pair and records the word and the match on the record sheet. That player then takes another turn.

4. If the cards do not match, the player returns the cards facedown.

5. The next player takes a turn and repeats steps 2–4.

6. Continue taking turns until all of the matches have been found.

What You NEED

✔ Vocabulary Memory Game Cards

✔ Vocabulary Memory Game Record Sheet

✔ Pencil or pen

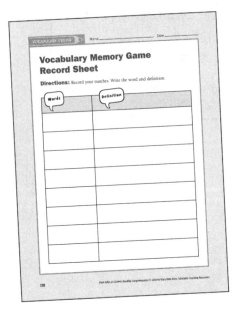

Hint! Hint!

Try to remember where the cards are so that you can match them.

Vocabulary Memory Game Cards

Name _____ Date _____

Vocabulary Memory Game Record Sheet

Directions: Record your matches. Write the word and definition.

Words	Definition

Word Charades

Description: Students dramatize vocabulary words as their classmates try to guess the words.

Materials

✤ Student directions (page 173)

✤ Word Charades Word Lists (page 174)

✤ Word Charades Word List Templates (page 175)

✤ Word Charades Record Sheets (page 176)

Procedures for Teaching

1. Display and read through the word lists. (Use the Word Charades Word List Templates to create new lists to reflect an area of study, if desired.) Point out that words in each list are grouped by categories, such as "Verbs" and "Feelings."

2. Explain to students how to demonstrate the meaning of a word by acting it out.

3. Choose a word (without telling students what it is) and act it out. Have students guess the word. When someone guesses correctly, confirm the guess by showing the word on the list.

4. Dramatize another word and have students write their guess on the record sheet. Demonstrate how to use the sheet, if necessary.

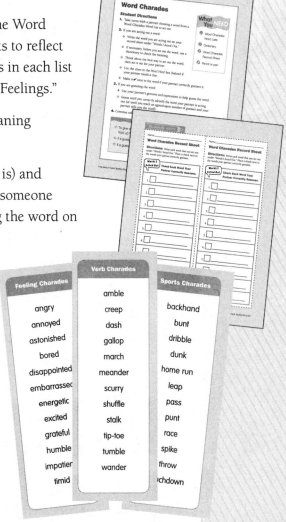

5. Invite a volunteer to dramatize a new word. Have students record and share answers.

6. Continue this process until students are comfortable with it.

7. For independent practice at the center, provide assorted word lists for students to choose from. Have students record the words they act out and guess correctly on a record sheet.

Suggestions for Differentiated Learning

Provide More Support

- Provide word lists with pictures.

- Let students work with partners to discuss the meaning of words and act them out.

- Start with more familiar words.

Provide More Challenge

- Have students write two or more possible words for each dramatization.

- Allow students to create additional word lists for charades. (See the Word Charades Word List Templates, page 175.)

Word Charades

Student Directions

What You NEED

✓ Word Charades Word Lists

✓ Dictionary

✓ Word Charades Record Sheet

✓ Pencil or pen

1. Take turns with a partner choosing a word from a Word Charades Word List to act out.

2. If you are acting out a word:

✤ Write the word you are acting out on your record sheet under "Words I Acted Out."

✤ If necessary, before you act out the word, use a dictionary to check the meaning.

✤ Think about the best way to act out the word, then act it out for your partner.

✤ Use the clues in the Hint! Hint! box (below) if your partner needs a clue.

✤ Make a ✔ next to the word if your partner correctly guesses it.

3. If you are guessing the word:

✤ Use your partner's gestures and expressions to help guess the word.

✤ Guess until you correctly identify the word your partner is acting out (or until you reach an agreed-upon number of guesses and your partner tells you the word).

4. Continue taking turns to act out and guess words.

Hint! Hint!

⇒ To give a clue about the word you are acting out, hold up fingers to show how many syllables.

⇒ If a guess is close, fan yourself to give the "warm" sign.

⇒ If a guess is not close, pretend to shiver to give the "cold" sign.

Word Charades Word Lists

Sports Charades

backhand

bunt

dribble

dunk

home run

leap

pass

punt

race

spike

throw

touchdown

Feeling Charades

angry

annoyed

astonished

bored

disappointed

embarrassed

energetic

excited

grateful

humble

impatient

timid

Verb Charades

amble

creep

dash

gallop

march

meander

scurry

shuffle

stalk

tip-toe

tumble

wander

Fresh Takes on Centers: Reading Comprehension © 2010 by Mary Beth Allen. Scholastic Teaching Resources

Word Charades Word List Templates

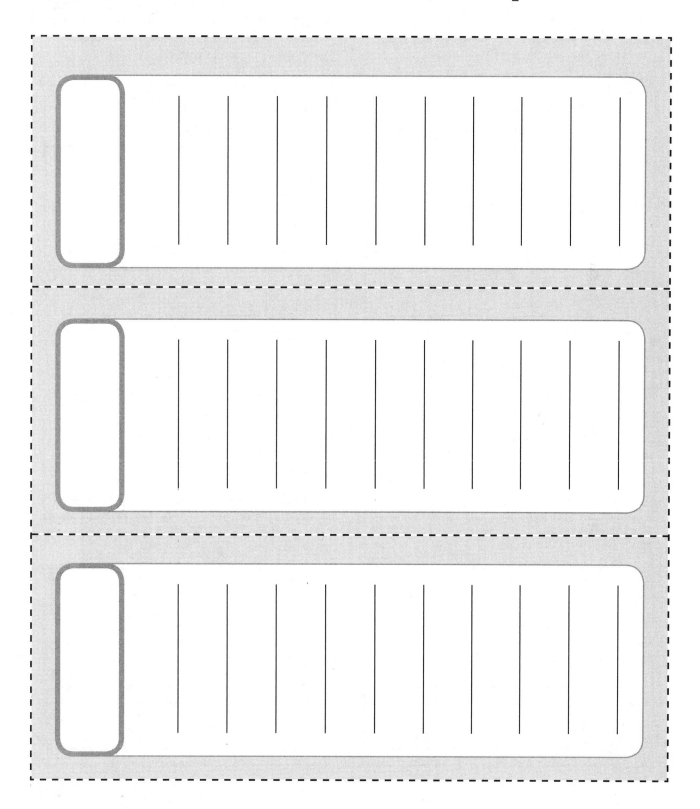

Name _____

Word Charades Record Sheet

Directions: Write each word that you act out under "Words I Acted Out." Place a check next to the words your partner correctly guesses.

Words I Acted Out	Check Each Word Your Partner Correctly Guesses.
1. ☐	_____
2. ☐	_____
3. ☐	_____
4. ☐	_____
5. ☐	_____
6. ☐	_____
7. ☐	_____
8. ☐	_____
9. ☐	_____
10. ☐	_____

Name _____

Word Charades Record Sheet

Directions: Write each word that you act out under "Words I Acted Out." Place a check next to the words your partner correctly guesses.

Words I Acted Out	Check Each Word Your Partner Correctly Guesses.
1. ☐	_____
2. ☐	_____
3. ☐	_____
4. ☐	_____
5. ☐	_____
6. ☐	_____
7. ☐	_____
8. ☐	_____
9. ☐	_____
10. ☐	_____

Fresh Takes on Centers: Reading Comprehension © 2010 by Mary Beth Allen. Scholastic Teaching Resources

Vocabulary Bingo

Description: Students match words and definitions, trying to fill in a row on the Bingo board.

Materials

✤ Student directions (page 179)

✤ Vocabulary Bingo Board (pages 180)

✤ Vocabulary Bingo Definition Cards (pages 181)

✤ Game Markers

✤ Bag (or small box)

Procedures for Teaching

1. To prepare, create a Bingo board for each student as follows: Using words from a set of 20 to 25 vocabulary words, fill in any 16 words in random order on each board. Create a definition card to match each word. Write the definition on one side and the vocabulary word on the reverse (or below the definition). Place all definition cards in a bag.

2. Review with students how to play Bingo. Then explain that in Vocabulary Bingo, the goal is to match words on the Bingo board with definitions.

3. Display a Bingo board. Randomly select a card and read the definition. Model how to look for and cover the matching word on the Bingo board. Think aloud about what different words on the board mean as you check for a match. If you have a match, show how to cover the word with a game marker. Then check the word on the definition card to make sure you are correct.

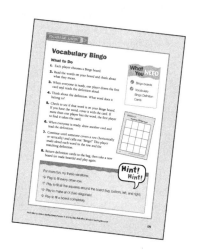

Teaching TIP

● Use vocabulary from content areas to create Bingo boards and definition cards.

● You may wish to laminate the definition cards for durability.

If the word is not on the board, confirm this and select a new card. Place definition cards in a pile as they are played.

4. As you continue, invite students to play with you. Repeat the process until you fill a row (horizontally, vertically, or diagonally) and call out "Bingo!" As you read aloud each word in turn, locate the matching definition card and reread the definition.

5. For independent practice, place Bingo boards and the bag of definition cards at the center. Have students play with partners or in small groups.

Teaching TIP

For variety, introduce other Bingo formations, including the following:

- Play to fill every other row.

- Play to fill the top, bottom, left side, and right side.

- Play to fill the entire board.

- Play to fill both diagonals (and make an X).

Suggestions for Differentiated Learning

Provide More Support

- Use a nine-square Bingo board (page 60).

- Have students match words with pictures.

- Provide word cards that include a sentence.

Provide More Challenge

- Use a 25-square Bingo board (page 62).

- Use a fill-in-the-blank format, synonyms, or antonyms instead of definitions.

- Have students play to cover more squares. (See Teaching Tip at left.)

Vocabulary Bingo

What to Do

1. Each player chooses a Bingo board. Read the words on your board and think about what they mean.

2. When everyone is ready, one player draws the first card and reads the definition aloud. Think about the definition. What word does it belong to?

3. Check to see if that word is on your Bingo board. If you have the word, cover it with a game marker. (More than one player can cover a space in each turn.) The player who read the definition calls out the word on the card. Players check to make sure they have correctly covered the word. Place definition cards in a pile as they are played.

4. When everyone is ready, draw another card and read the definition.

5. Continue until someone covers a row (horizontally or vertically) and calls out "Bingo!" This player reads aloud each word in the row, finds the matching definition card, and rereads the definition.

6. Return definition cards to the bag, then take a new board (or trade boards) and play again.

What You NEED

- ✔ Bingo boards
- ✔ Vocabulary Bingo Definition Cards

Hint! Hint!

For more fun, try these variations:

⇒ Play to fill every other row.

⇒ Play to fill all the squares around the board (top, bottom, left, and right).

⇒ Play to make an X (two diagonals).

⇒ Play to fill a board completely.

Vocabulary Bingo Board

Vocabulary Bingo Definition Cards

Vocabulary Bingo Definition Cards	**Vocabulary Bingo Definition Cards**	**Vocabulary Bingo Definition Cards**	**Vocabulary Bingo Definition Cards**
Vocabulary Bingo Definition Cards	**Vocabulary Bingo Definition Cards**	**Vocabulary Bingo Definition Cards**	**Vocabulary Bingo Definition Cards**
Vocabulary Bingo Definition Cards	**Vocabulary Bingo Definition Cards**	**Vocabulary Bingo Definition Cards**	**Vocabulary Bingo Definition Cards**
Vocabulary Bingo Definition Cards	**Vocabulary Bingo Definition Cards**	**Vocabulary Bingo Definition Cards**	**Vocabulary Bingo Definition Cards**

Synonym Riddles

Description: Students play with word meanings by writing riddles related to pairs of words.

Materials

✤ Riddle books

✤ Student directions (page 184)

✤ Synonym Riddles Planning Sheets (page 185)

✤ Dictionary, thesaurus, and rhyming dictionary

Procedures for Teaching

1. Display several riddle books and share some riddles with students.

2. Model the process for creating rhymes called "Hink Pinks" using the Synonym Riddles Planning Sheet.

3. To create a Hink-Pink riddle, start by identifying two rhyming words, such as *small* and *ball*.

4. Suggest a synonym for each word—for example, *tiny* and *sphere*. Model using a thesaurus or dictionary, if necessary.

5. Insert the synonyms into the question: "What do you call a/an _____ _____?" The answer is, of course, the rhyming pair.

6. Give students another pair of rhyming words and have them create a riddle.

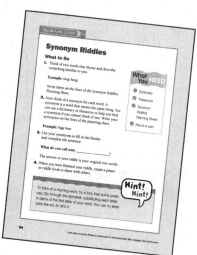

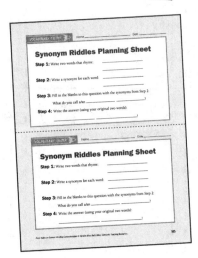

7. In pairs or small groups, have students create another example and share with the class. Provide support with generating rhyming word pairs and synonyms, as needed.

8. For independent practice, have students use the Synonym Riddles Planning Sheets at the center to create new riddles, then make posters or riddle books for others to enjoy.

How to Make a "Layer" Book

1. Stack several sheets of paper together and position them vertically. Beginning with the second to last sheet, slide each sheet up and away from the one below by about one inch.

2. Holding the paper securely, fold the top down toward the opposite end, and stop about an inch from the first sheet.

3. Crease at the fold and staple to bind.

Teaching ↘ TIP

"Layer" books make excellent vehicles for publishing students' riddle books (see left).

Suggestions for Differentiated Learning

Provide More Support

- Provide sets of rhyming words. Have students generate synonyms to create the riddle.

- Provide completed riddles and sets of rhyming words. Have students locate the answers to the riddles.

Provide More Challenge

- Use multisyllabic words (such as *funny bunny*).

- Use other types of word pairs, such as homonyms (*sail* and *sale*) and oxymorons (*large shrimp*).

Synonym Riddles

What to Do

1. Think of two words that rhyme and describe something familiar to you.

 Example: *large barge*

 Write them on the lines of the Synonym Riddles Planning Sheet.

2. Now think of a synonym for each word. A synonym is a word that means the same thing. You can use a dictionary or thesaurus to help you find a synonym if you cannot think of one. Write your synonyms on the lines of the planning sheet.

 Example: *huge boat*

3. Use your synonyms to fill in the blanks and complete the sentence:

 What do you call a/an _____ _____?

 The answer to your riddle is your original two words.

4. When you have finished your riddle, create a poster or riddle book to share with others.

What You NEED

- ✓ Dictionary
- ✓ Thesaurus
- ✓ Synonym Riddles Planning Sheet
- ✓ Pencil or pen

To think of a rhyming word, try a trick that some poets use. Go through the alphabet, substituting each letter in place of the first letter of your word. You can try letter pairs like *sw*, *br*, and *tr*.

Name _____ Date _____

Synonym Riddles Planning Sheet

Step 1: Write two words that rhyme: _____

_____

Step 2: Write a synonym for each word: _____

_____

Step 3: Fill in the blanks to this question with the synonyms from Step 2:

What do you call a/an _____ _____?

Step 4: Write the answer (using your original two words):

_____ _____!

Name _____ Date _____

Synonym Riddles Planning Sheet

Step 1: Write two words that rhyme: _____

_____

Step 2: Write a synonym for each word: _____

_____

Step 3: Fill in the blanks to this question with the synonyms from Step 2:

What do you call a/an _____ _____?

Step 4: Write the answer (using your original two words):

_____ _____!

Vocabulary Scavenger Hunt

Description: Students use clues to find specific vocabulary words in a short text or poem.

Materials

✤ Short stories or poems

✤ Student directions (page 188)

✤ Vocabulary Scavenger Hunt Record Sheets (pages 189–190)

Procedures for Teaching

1. Choose a short, familiar text to share. Fill in the blanks on a Vocabulary Scavenger Hunt Record Sheet based on that text. Introduce the concept of the scavenger hunt and explain to students that you will be reading clues and then trying to find words those clues describe in the text you are reading.

2. Display a short story or poem (or other short text). Read it aloud to students. Then have them join in and read it with you.

3. Display the Vocabulary Scavenger Hunt Record Sheet. Review terminology, such as the words *antonym*, *adjective*, and *root*.

4. Model finding the first word on the scavenger hunt. Share your thought process aloud as you look for the correct word.

5. Read the next clue and have the students help you find the word in the text.

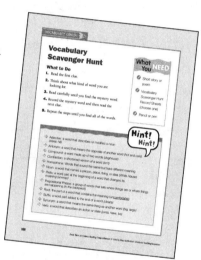

6. Continue the process, inviting students to explain what they know about the clues (such as *prefix*, *suffix*, and *contraction*), and gradually release responsibility to pairs or small groups of students.

7. For independent practice at the center, display a poem or other short text, or provide copies for each student to read. Customize the Vocabulary Scavenger Hunt Record Sheet based on the text or use it as a model to create your own scavenger hunt for specific words in the text.

Suggestions for Differentiated Learning

Provide More Support

- Use shorter or more familiar poems or texts.

- Focus on one type of word, for example, synonyms. (Create a simplified scavenger hunt in this case.)

Provide More Challenge

- Use more challenging or longer texts.

- Have students choose a poem and create their own scavenger hunt for classmates to use.

- Create a scavenger hunt that has students find examples of literary or poetic devices, such as metaphor and alliteration.

Vocabulary Scavenger Hunt

What to Do

1. Read the first clue.

2. Think about what kind of word you are looking for.

3. Read carefully until you find the mystery word.

4. Record the mystery word and then read the next clue.

5. Repeat the steps until you find all of the words.

What You NEED

- ✓ Short story or poem
- ✓ Vocabulary Scavenger Hunt Record Sheets (choose one)
- ✓ Pencil or pen

Hint! Hint!

⇒ **Adjective:** a word that describes or modifies a noun (*steep hill*)

⇒ **Antonym:** a word that means the opposite of another word (*hot* and *cold*)

⇒ **Compound:** a word made up of two words (*doghouse*)

⇒ **Contraction:** a shortened version of a word (*isn't*)

⇒ **Homophones:** words that sound the same but have different meaning

⇒ **Noun:** a word that names a person, place, thing, or idea (*White House*)

⇒ **Prefix:** a word part at the beginning of a word that changes its meaning (*unwrap*)

⇒ **Prepositional Phrase:** a group of words that tells where things are or where things are happening (*in the backpack*)

⇒ **Root:** the part of a word that contains the meaning (un*comfortable*)

⇒ **Suffix:** a word part added to the end of a word (*clearly*)

⇒ **Synonym:** a word that means the same thing as another word (*big, large*)

⇒ **Verb:** a word that describes an action or state (*jump, have, be*)

Fresh Takes on Centers: Reading Comprehension © 2010 by Mary Beth Allen. Scholastic Teaching Resources

Name _____ Date _____

Vocabulary Scavenger Hunt Record Sheet

Clues	Answers
1 A word that means _____	
2 An antonym of _____	
3 A synonym of _____	
4 A word that rhymes with _____	
5 A compound word	
6 A two-syllable word	
7 A contraction	
8 A noun	

Name _____   Date _____

Vocabulary Scavenger Hunt Record Sheet

Clues	Answers
1 A word that means _____ _____.	
2 An antonym of _____	
3 An adjective	
4 A word with a prefix	
5 A word with a suffix	
6 A word with a root that means _____.	
7 A word that describes _____.	
8 A prepositional phrase	
9 A contraction	
10 A homophone	

Fresh Takes on Centers: Reading Comprehension © 2010 by Mary Beth Allen. Scholastic Teaching Resources

References

Allington, R. (2005). The other five "pillars" of effective reading instruction. *Reading Today, 22*(6), 3.

Beaver, J. M. (2006). *Developmental reading assessment: Grades K–3* (2nd ed.). Parsipanny, NJ: Pearson Education.

Beaver, J. M., & Carter, M. A. (2003). *Developmental reading assessment: Grades 4–8.* Parsipanny, NJ: Pearson Education.

Brown, R. (2008). The road not yet taken: A transactional strategies approach to comprehension instruction. *The Reading Teacher, 61*(7), 538–547.

Diller, D. (2007). *Making the most of small groups: Differentiation for all.* Portland, ME: Stenhouse.

Duke, N. K., & Pearson, P. D. (2002). Effective practices for developing reading comprehension. In A. E. Farstrup & S. J. Samuels (Eds.), *What research has to say about reading instruction* (pp. 205–242). Newark, DE: International Reading Association.

Durkin, D. (1978–1979). What classroom observations reveal about reading comprehension instruction. *Reading Research Quarterly, 14*(4), 481–533.

Estes, T. H., & Johnstone, J. P. (1977). Twelve easy ways to make readers hate reading (and one difficult way to make them love it). *Language Arts, 54*(8), 891–897.

Fielding, L., & Pearson, P. D. (1994). Reading comprehension: What works. *Educational Leadership, 51*(5), 62–68.

Fountas, I., & Pinnell, G. (2007). Fountas and Pinnell Benchmark Assessment System 2 (Grades 3–8). Portsmouth, NH: Heinemann.

Fountas, I., & Pinnell, G. (1996). *Guided reading: Good first teaching for all children.* Portsmouth, NH: Heinemann.

Gambrell, L. B., Malloy, J. A., & Mazzoni, S. A. (2007). Evidence-based best practices for comprehensive literacy instruction. In Gambrell, L. B., Morrow, L. M. M. & Pressley, M. (Eds.), *Best practices in literacy instruction* (3rd ed.) (pp. 11–29). New York: Guilford.

Harvey, S., & Goudvis, A. (2007). *Strategies that work: Teaching comprehension for understanding and engagement*. Portland, ME: Stenhouse.

Keene, E. O., & Zimmermann, S. (2007). *Mosaic of thought: The power of comprehension strategy instruction* (2nd ed.). Portsmouth, NH: Heinemann.

McLaughlin, M., & Allen, M. B. (2002). *Guided comprehension: A teaching model for grades 3–8*. Newark, DE: International Reading Association.

National Institute of Child Health and Human Development (NICHHD). (2000). *Report of the National Reading Panel. Teaching children to read: An evidence-based assessment of the scientific research literature on reading and its implications for reading instruction* (NIH Publication No. 00-4769). Washington, DC: U.S. Government Printing Office.

Pressley, M., Wharton-McDonald, R., Mistretta-Hampston, J., & Echevarria, M. (1998). Literacy instruction in 10 fourth- and fifth-grade classrooms in upstate New York. *Scientific Studies of Reading, 2*(2), 159–194.

Reutzel, D. R., Smith, J. A., & Fawson, P. C. (2005). An evaluation of two approaches for teaching reading comprehension strategies in the primary years using science information texts. *Early Childhood Research Quarterly, 20*(3), 276–305.

Tyner, B., & Green, S. E. (2005). *Small-group reading instruction: A differentiated teaching model for intermediate readers, grades 3-8*. Newark, DE: International Reading Association.